Relational Leadership

Empowering People for Global Impact

Relational Leadership

Empowering People for Global Impact

Louis Adam

EXCELLER BOOKS®
A GLOBAL PRESS

Relational Leadership

Empowering People for Global Impact

Cover by Exceller Books using resources from Pixabay.com

ISBN: 978-93-48892-67-6

First published in India in 2025 by Exceller Books,
An imprint of GE Group,
G1, Dream Apartment, Degree College Road, Belgharia,
Kolkata, 700056, India
www.excellerbooks.com

EXCELLER BOOKS®
A GLOBAL PRESS

Dedication

To my beloved wife, Dr. Eugenia Tawiah Adam, whose unwavering love, encouragement, and partnership have been the cornerstone of my life and ministry.

To my children—Nathaniel, Naysa, and Nadav—whose lives inspire me to be a better leader and father every day.

To every leader seeking to make a lasting impact through relationships: may this book equip and encourage you to lead with wisdom, compassion, and authenticity.

Acknowledgment

I am deeply grateful to God Almighty, whose grace and guidance have been the foundation of my life and ministry.

To my spiritual family at Harvest Chapel International—thank you for your prayers, support, and trust in my leadership. Special mention to our Bishop, Rev. Fitzgerald Odonkor, under whose tutelage I have learned to do ministry; Rev. Emmanuel Titti Lartey and Rev. Kwesi Dickson—God bless you for being a support.

To Mr. and Mrs. Addo-Ayis, Mrs. Philomena Gyamfi, Mr. and Mrs. Nyarko Mensah, Mr. and Mrs. Aidoo (USA), Prophet Andrew Mensah (USA), and Dr. Selom Kwame Adatsi (USA)—thank you for your great support and encouragement.

To my wife, Dr. Eugenia Tawiah Adam—your steadfast love and encouragement have been my greatest source of strength.

To our children, Nathaniel, Naysa, and Nadav—you are our greatest joy and motivation.

To all mentors, colleagues, and friends who have shaped my journey—thank you for your invaluable insights and support. This book is a tribute to all who inspire and lead with love.

Table of Contents

Leadership Thrives Through Relationships: A Global Perspective

Foundational Scripture: Exodus 18:1–27

Introduction

Leadership is a universal and timeless phenomenon. Across cultures, nations, and industries, leaders play a crucial role in shaping the future of organizations, communities, and societies. Despite the vast differences in leadership styles across the globe, one key element remains consistent: the power of relationships. Whether leading in a corporation, a nonprofit organization, a nation, or a family, strong, meaningful relationships are the bedrock of enduring leadership.

This book, *Leadership Thrives through Relationships*, draws from the timeless wisdom found in Exodus 18:1–27, where Moses, one of history's most renowned leaders, receives crucial advice from his father-in-law, Jethro. Jethro's counsel helps Moses restructure his leadership approach, prioritizing relationships and delegation, which in turn leads to a more effective and sustainable leadership model.

In this book, we will unpack the lessons from this foundational biblical text and apply them to the modern, global leadership landscape. Whether you are leading in business, government, or a community organization, the principles of relational leadership presented here will provide valuable insights into how to lead with influence, build trust, and create lasting impact.

|Chapter 1|

The Foundation of Relational Leadership

Exodus 18:16 – The Power of Connection

Leadership begins with relationships, and at the heart of every successful leader is a deep understanding of people. In Exodus 18, the relationship between Moses and Jethro serves as a model for how great leaders rely on trusted relationships for advice, encouragement, and support. Jethro, who is both a priest and Moses' father-in-law, recognizes that Moses is overburdened by the demands of leadership and provides him with advice that not only relieves his stress but also strengthens his leadership.

In a global context, leaders face diverse and complex challenges that require them to build networks of support, advice, and collaboration. This chapter explores how relational leadership—rooted in connection and mentorship—is crucial for long-term success. It will cover:

- **Why relationships are central to leadership success**: Just as Jethro saw Moses struggling and offered guidance, modern leaders must recognize the importance of building networks of mentors and advisors. In a globalized world, leaders need to foster relationships across cultures and industries to gather insights, collaborate, and innovate.
- **The importance of humility and openness**: Moses' willingness to listen to Jethro is a powerful example of

the humility that leaders must exhibit. Leadership isn't about knowing everything; it's about being open to learning from others and fostering an environment where guidance and feedback are welcomed.

- **The role of mentorship in leadership**: The global leadership environment is increasingly diverse, requiring leaders to mentor and be mentored by those from different cultural, generational, and professional backgrounds. This chapter will explore how leaders can build mentoring relationships that foster growth for both the mentor and mentee.

|Chapter 2|

Identifying and Empowering Others

Exodus 18:17–23 – The Principle of Delegation

One of the most critical pieces of advice Jethro gives Moses is to delegate responsibilities to capable individuals. He tells Moses, *"What you are doing is not good. You and these people who come to you will only wear yourselves out"* (Exodus 18:17–18). Jethro's insight shows that leadership is not about doing everything yourself but about empowering others to lead alongside you.

This chapter dives into the importance of delegation as a key component of relational leadership. In the modern, fast-paced global environment, leaders cannot succeed by micromanaging or holding onto control. Instead, they must learn to delegate tasks, trust others, and build teams that share the burden of leadership. Topics include:

- **The benefits of empowering others**: Just as Jethro instructed Moses to appoint capable men to serve as leaders of groups, today's leaders must identify and empower individuals within their organizations. By delegating tasks, leaders create space for others to grow and contribute their strengths.
- **Building trust through delegation**: Delegation is not just about offloading tasks; it's about trusting others to carry out responsibilities effectively. This requires

building strong relationships with those you lead so they feel empowered and confident in their roles.

- **The global challenge of delegation**: In a diverse and global workforce, leaders must recognize the value of cross-cultural delegation. This means understanding the unique strengths and perspectives of individuals from different cultural backgrounds and giving them opportunities to lead within their areas of expertise.

|Chapter 3|

Sustainable Leadership for a Global World

Exodus 18:13–16 – Leading with Wisdom and Balance

Before Jethro intervened, Moses was overworking himself by handling every dispute and problem that arose among the Israelites. He was trying to be everything for everyone, which made his leadership unsustainable. Jethro's counsel to Moses highlighted the need for leaders to have balance and wisdom in how they manage their responsibilities.

In the modern world, the challenges of leadership are greater than ever before. Global leaders must deal with economic uncertainty, technological disruptions, cultural differences, and the growing demand for sustainable practices. This chapter explores the principles of wisdom and balance in leadership, using Moses' story as a guide. Topics include:

- **Avoiding leadership burnout**: Moses' attempt to do everything alone led him to the brink of burnout, a common challenge for today's leaders. Leaders must learn how to prioritize their tasks, delegate effectively, and create healthy boundaries to ensure long-term sustainability.
- **The role of wisdom in decision-making**: Jethro's advice to Moses was rooted in wisdom, which helped Moses shift from a reactive leader to a proactive one. Leaders today must cultivate wisdom by seeking diverse perspectives, learning from experience, and

making informed decisions that consider long-term impact.

- **Global sustainability and leadership**: Just as Moses had to restructure his leadership to be sustainable, modern leaders must adopt strategies that promote sustainability within their organizations and the environment. This includes developing eco-friendly practices, fostering a culture of well-being, and addressing global challenges with foresight and responsibility.

|Chapter 4|

Creating a Culture of Collaboration

Exodus 18:21–23 – Leadership through Teams

Jethro's advice to Moses included appointing leaders over groups of thousands, hundreds, fifties, and tens. This structure allowed for more efficient management and created a culture of collaboration, where leadership was distributed, and people were empowered to solve problems at different levels.

This chapter explores the importance of creating a culture of collaboration in global leadership. Whether you are leading a multinational corporation or a small community group, collaboration is key to success. We'll discuss:

- **Building collaborative teams**: In the global workplace, leaders must build teams that work together effectively, leveraging the strengths of each member. This includes fostering open communication, encouraging creativity, and creating an environment where collaboration is valued over competition.
- **Leading diverse teams**: The global nature of leadership means that leaders must understand how to work with teams composed of individuals from different cultural, linguistic, and professional backgrounds. We'll explore strategies for navigating cultural differences and fostering inclusion in the workplace.

- **The role of technology in collaboration**: With advancements in technology, leaders have more tools than ever to foster collaboration across time zones and geographies. This section will explore how leaders can use technology to enhance collaboration and communication in a global context.

|Chapter 5|

The Role of Emotional Intelligence in Global Leadership

Exodus 18:23 – Leading with Empathy and Understanding

Jethro's advice was not only practical but also rooted in a deep understanding of Moses' emotional and physical limits. He cared about Moses' well-being and the well-being of the people Moses was leading. This care and concern reflect the importance of emotional intelligence in leadership.

In today's interconnected and often volatile global environment, emotional intelligence (EQ) is a critical skill for leaders. Leaders with high emotional intelligence can navigate complex interpersonal relationships, understand the emotional needs of their team members, and lead with empathy. This chapter focuses on:

- **The five components of emotional intelligence:** Self-awareness, self-regulation, motivation, empathy, and social skills are all critical to leading effectively. Leaders who develop these qualities are better equipped to connect with their teams, manage conflict, and foster a positive organizational culture.
- **Leading with empathy in a global context:** As leaders work with people from various cultural and socioeconomic backgrounds, empathy becomes even more important. Understanding the challenges and emotions of

individuals from different walks of life helps build trust and loyalty.

- **How emotional intelligence drives performance:** Research shows that leaders with high emotional intelligence are more effective in managing teams, improving performance, and increasing employee satisfaction. We'll explore how global leaders can develop and leverage emotional intelligence to inspire and motivate those they lead.

|Chapter 6|

Building Lasting Legacies through Relationships

Exodus 18:24–27 – Leadership That Endures

Moses implemented Jethro's advice, and the results were transformative. Not only did Moses find relief, but the people he led were better served, and new leaders emerged. The changes Moses made allowed him to focus on his core responsibilities and created a legacy of leadership that endured long after him.

This final chapter explores how relational leadership builds legacies that last. Leaders who invest in relationships, delegate wisely, and foster collaboration create environments where leadership can thrive for generations. Topics include:

- **Mentoring the next generation of leaders:** Just as Moses empowered others to lead, global leaders must focus on mentoring and developing the next generation of leaders. We'll discuss how to build mentoring relationships that prepare future leaders for the challenges of a globalized world.
- **Leaving a leadership legacy:** The legacy of a leader is not measured solely by achievements but by the future. This section will explore how leaders can create succession plans that ensure continuity and preserve the values of relational leadership.

Conclusion: Global Leadership through Relationships

Leadership is a global phenomenon, and its principles are universal. No matter where you are in the world, relationships are at the core of effective leadership. By applying the lessons from Moses and Jethro, leaders today can build trust, empower others, and lead sustainably in an increasingly complex and interconnected world.

This book has explored how relational leadership not only enhances the well-being of the leader but also benefits the people they serve. As you continue your leadership journey, remember that true leadership is not about exerting control but about building meaningful, lasting relationships that create value, foster growth, and leave a lasting legacy.

Would you like to expand on any particular chapter or add more practical examples?

Exodus 18:16 – The Power of Connection

Leadership is fundamentally about relationships. No matter the size of an organization, the nature of a community, or the global reach of a company, leadership is not a solo endeavor. It's about connecting with people, understanding their needs, and guiding them toward a common goal. The story of Moses and Jethro in Exodus 18 provides us with timeless wisdom on the power of connection and how relationships form the bedrock of sustainable, impactful leadership.

In Exodus 18, Moses, who had led the Israelites out of Egypt, was now faced with the overwhelming responsibility of managing and leading a vast group of people. The daily demands on his leadership were exhausting him, and it was affecting his ability to serve his people effectively. When Jethro, his father-in-law, came to visit, he observed Moses' leadership style and noticed that Moses was carrying the entire burden alone. This chapter begins with Jethro's arrival and their relational interaction, which sets the stage for one of the most critical leadership lessons: the necessity of building connections and seeking wise counsel.

Jethro's insight and advice to Moses teach us that leadership thrives when leaders are willing to connect, collaborate, and share the weight of responsibility with others. His role as both a mentor and family member demonstrates the importance of having trusted relationships in leadership—people who can offer wisdom, challenge us, and support us through difficult decisions.

The Importance of Relationships in Leadership

Leadership is not a one-dimensional role. While it often involves vision, strategy, and decision-making, the effectiveness of a leader is ultimately measured by their ability to influence and inspire people. This influence is deeply rooted in relationships.

Jethro's relationship with Moses was not just familial; it was built on mutual respect and trust. Jethro's wisdom as a priest and elder positioned him to offer valuable counsel to Moses. Moses, in turn, was humble enough to listen. This dynamic highlights a critical principle in leadership: leaders need trusted relationships to succeed. A leader cannot lead in isolation, nor can they rely solely on their own knowledge or expertise.

The global leadership landscape, whether in business, politics, or community organizations, is no different today. The most successful leaders are those who have built strong networks of trusted advisors, mentors, and collaborators. They understand that leadership is a relational endeavor, and without the support and input of others, even the most talented leaders can quickly become overwhelmed.

Building Networks of Trust

One of the first lessons we learn from Moses and Jethro's interaction is the value of building networks of trust. Moses' leadership, though powerful, was limited because he had not yet structured his leadership in a way that allowed others to help carry the burden. Jethro saw this and immediately understood that Moses needed to delegate responsibility and empower others.

In a globalized world, leaders must build networks of trust both within and outside their organizations. These networks often span across cultural, geographical, and industry boundaries, allowing leaders to gather diverse perspectives and ideas. Trust is the foundation of these relationships, and it is built through:

1. **Consistent Communication** – Leaders who are transparent and communicate openly with their teams foster trust. Consistent communication builds confidence and ensures that everyone is aligned with the organization's vision and goals. In the story of Moses, Jethro's candid communication about the inefficiencies in Moses' leadership was rooted in their trust-based relationship.
2. **Integrity and Reliability** – Trust is built when leaders demonstrate integrity in their actions and decisions. People follow leaders they can rely on—leaders who keep their promises, admit their mistakes, and lead by

example. Moses' willingness to listen to Jethro's counsel and implement his advice showed his integrity as a leader.

3. **Mutual Respect** – Trust cannot exist without respect. Leaders who value the input and perspectives of others, regardless of their position, create an environment where trust can flourish. Jethro's relationship with Moses was rooted in mutual respect, allowing Jethro to offer advice and Moses to receive it without defensiveness.

Building networks of trust allows leaders to leverage the strengths of others, make better decisions, and create a more collaborative leadership environment.

Humility in Leadership: A Key to Relational Success

A major theme in Exodus 18 is Moses' humility. Despite being the leader of an entire nation, Moses didn't act with arrogance or self-sufficiency. When Jethro pointed out that his leadership structure was unsustainable, Moses didn't dismiss the advice; he listened and was willing to make changes. This kind of humility is critical in leadership because it opens the door for collaboration, growth, and meaningful relationships.

In a global context, leaders are increasingly required to navigate complex, cross-cultural environments. The most effective leaders are those who are humble enough to admit that they don't have all the answers. They seek out input from others, especially from those with different perspectives and experiences. This openness to learning fosters a culture of innovation and inclusion, where people feel valued and empowered to contribute.

The Global Challenge of Humility

In many cultures, leadership is associated with authority and control. However, leaders who cling to these outdated notions of leadership risk isolating themselves and alienating their teams. The global nature of modern leadership demands a more nuanced, relational approach—one that values humility and the willingness to learn from others.

Moses could have easily dismissed Jethro's advice, but his humility allowed him to recognize that Jethro's counsel would benefit both him and the people he led. This teaches modern leaders that humility is not a weakness; it is a strength. Leaders who are humble enough to acknowledge their limitations and seek advice from others are more likely to succeed in the long term.

The Role of Mentorship in Leadership Development

Jethro's role in Moses' life was that of a mentor—someone who provided wisdom, guidance, and perspective. Mentorship is a critical component of relational leadership. Just as Moses needed Jethro's guidance to help restructure his leadership, modern leaders need mentors to help them navigate the complexities of leadership.

Mentors offer a safe space for leaders to express their challenges, fears, and uncertainties. They provide objective insights and share their experiences to help guide decision-making. In a global context, mentorship can transcend borders, with leaders seeking out mentors from different industries, cultures, or geographical regions to gain broader perspectives.

How to Build Effective Mentoring Relationships

1. **Seek Out Wise Counsel** – Just as Jethro brought wisdom from his experience as a priest and elder, leaders should actively seek out mentors with deep experience and knowledge. These mentors can provide invaluable insights that help leaders avoid common pitfalls and develop their leadership skills.
2. **Commit to Lifelong Learning** – Moses' willingness to learn from Jethro, despite his significant leadership role, shows that great leaders are lifelong learners. Leaders who embrace continuous learning through mentorship are better equipped to handle the evolving challenges of leadership in a globalized world.
3. **Invest in Mentoring Others** – Just as Moses benefited from Jethro's mentorship, leaders must also invest in mentoring the next generation of leaders. This creates a cycle of growth and development, ensuring that leadership knowledge and wisdom are passed on.

Building Relational Leadership in a Global Context

The lessons from Moses and Jethro are not limited to the context of ancient Israel. They apply just as powerfully to modern global leadership. In a world where leaders face complex challenges—ranging from technological disruption to cross-cultural collaboration—relational leadership is more important than ever.

The following are key principles for building relational leadership on a global scale:

Foster Cross-Cultural Relationships: As leaders work across borders and with diverse teams, they must prioritize building relationships that transcend cultural differences. Understanding cultural nuances, respecting diverse perspectives, and fostering inclusivity are key components of relational leadership in a global context.

Develop Emotional Intelligence: Relational leadership requires leaders to be emotionally intelligent. This means being aware of their own emotions and the emotions of others and using that awareness to navigate interpersonal relationships effectively. Leaders with high emotional intelligence are better equipped to lead diverse teams and handle the challenges of global leadership.

Create a Collaborative Leadership Structure: Just as Moses needed to delegate and empower others to lead alongside him, global leaders must create collaborative leadership structures. This involves sharing power, trusting others, and building teams that work together toward a common goal.

Conclusion: The Foundation of Leadership Is Relationships

In Exodus 18, the relationship between Moses and Jethro provides us with a powerful example of how leadership thrives on relationships. Moses was an extraordinary leader, but without Jethro's counsel, his leadership could have faltered. The wisdom, trust, and humility present in their relationship helped Moses become a more effective and sustainable leader.

For leaders today, the lesson is clear: leadership is not about doing everything yourself or relying solely on your own abilities. It is about building strong, meaningful relationships with those around you—mentors, advisers, and the people you lead. By investing in relationships, leaders can foster collaboration, create sustainable leadership structures, and ultimately lead with greater impact in an increasingly complex global world.

The foundation of relational leadership is simple: connect with others, build trust, and lead with humility. When these elements are in place, leadership becomes not only more effective but also more fulfilling—for both the leader and those they serve.

1. Connecting with Others

The first step in relational leadership is connection. Leaders who genuinely connect with people build bridges that foster understanding, empathy, and solidarity. These connections transcend hierarchical boundaries and foster a sense of belonging. By reaching out, a leader shows they are approachable, which opens the door to candid communication. Such connections are essential because they make people feel seen, valued, and part of something larger. When leaders engage in this way, they create a collaborative environment where people feel free to contribute, making the team and the organization stronger as a whole.

This initial connection isn't just about formal interactions; it often extends to informal conversations, shared experiences, and genuine concern for each individual's well-being. Leaders who connect with others gain invaluable insights into their motivations, fears, and aspirations, allowing them to tailor their leadership approach accordingly. Effective relational leaders don't just understand the work; they understand the people behind it.

2. Building Trust

Trust is the backbone of any relationship, and it's no different in leadership. When trust is established, it fosters a safe environment where people are willing to be vulnerable, open, and honest. They know that they are in a space where their contributions are respected and their shortcomings are not a source of ridicule. Trust is a two-way street: just as team members need to trust their leader, the leader must also demonstrate trust in their team's abilities and judgment.

Trust-building is an ongoing effort and requires consistency, transparency, and reliability. Leaders who keep their promises, communicate openly, and support their team even in challenging times are more likely to gain lasting trust. Once established, trust allows leaders to guide their teams through challenges with the knowledge that everyone is aligned and committed to the same goals. A high-trust environment is marked by resilience, as people feel empowered to take calculated risks and push their creative boundaries, knowing their leader supports their growth and has their back.

3. Leading with Humility

Humility is one of the most transformative qualities a leader can have. Humble leaders recognize that they don't have all the answers and are willing to listen, learn, and adapt. Humility allows a leader to remain open to feedback, which is essential for personal and professional growth. This quality breaks down barriers, allowing the leader to genuinely learn from their team and recognize the strengths each person brings. A humble leader admits mistakes and is open about their own areas of improvement, which encourages team members to adopt a similar attitude of growth and resilience. Leading with humility means prioritizing the well-being and success of the team over personal gain. Humility positions the leader as a servant, committed to uplifting and empowering others. This approach fosters a nurturing and collaborative atmosphere where everyone feels a shared responsibility for success.

The Power of Relational Leadership in Action

When these elements—connection, trust, and humility—come together, leadership becomes a relationship-building endeavor. Leaders who practice relational leadership understand that people follow people, not titles or positions. When a leader invests time in building relationships, they create a solid foundation for loyalty and dedication. People are more likely to go above and beyond when they feel truly valued and supported.

The fulfillment in relational leadership comes from the shared journey and mutual growth. Leaders find joy not just in the accomplishments but in watching their team members grow, take ownership, and succeed. For people, having a leader who cares about their growth and well-being makes the work more than just a job; it becomes a journey of personal and collective achievement.

Benefits of Relational Leadership

1. **Increased Engagement and Motivation:** Relational leadership drives engagement because it appeals to

the human need for connection. When people feel connected to their leader and peers, they are more likely to be engaged in their work.

2. **Better Conflict Resolution**: In a high-trust environment where people feel safe, conflicts can be addressed openly and constructively. Relational leaders resolve conflicts through empathy and understanding, ensuring all parties feel heard and respected.
3. **Higher Performance and Retention**: Teams with strong relational bonds are more cohesive and perform better because they operate on shared values and trust. Relational leaders see higher retention rates, as employees are more likely to stay where they feel valued and respected.

In Summary: Leadership Thrives on Relationships

Leadership at its core is about service, and relational leadership brings this to life by centering on genuine connections, trust, and humility. When a leader fosters a culture based on these principles, they create an environment where people feel respected, empowered, and motivated. Relational leadership is not only effective but deeply fulfilling, as it creates spaces where everyone can thrive, grow, and feel part of a meaningful purpose. Leadership indeed thrives on relationships because relationships are what bring the mission, vision, and purpose of an organization to life.

|Chapter 7|

Identifying and Empowering Others

Exodus 18:17-23 – The Principle of Delegation

In the fast-paced, increasingly complex world of leadership, one of the greatest challenges leaders face is the temptation to carry the entire burden on their own shoulders. Whether leading a small team or overseeing a global organization, leaders often find themselves overwhelmed by the demands of their roles, feeling the need to solve every problem and make every decision. This is exactly where Moses found himself in Exodus 18, managing the day-to-day concerns of an entire nation alone.

When Jethro saw this, he quickly recognized the danger. He knew that no leader, no matter how capable or talented, could succeed without empowering others. Jethro's advice to Moses is one of the most powerful examples in the Bible of the importance of delegation: "What you are doing is not good. You and these people who come to you will only wear yourselves out. The work is too heavy for you; you cannot handle it alone" (Exodus 18:17-18).

Jethro's words serve as a timeless reminder for leaders across the globe: leadership is not about doing everything yourself; it's about empowering others to share the load. This chapter delves into the principle of delegation and how identifying and empowering others is a crucial part of relational leadership.

The Burden of Trying to Do It All

Moses, like many modern leaders, was caught in a cycle of exhaustion and inefficiency. As the leader of the Israelites, he felt responsible for addressing every dispute, hearing every case, and making every decision. While his intentions were good, his method was unsustainable. The workload was simply too much for one person to bear, and it was beginning to take its toll—not only on Moses but also on the people waiting for his judgment.

Jethro's intervention was timely. He identified that Moses' approach was detrimental not only to his health and effectiveness as a leader but also to the overall well-being of the community he was leading. Jethro's counsel to Moses was simple yet profound: delegate authority to others who are capable and trustworthy.

In today's global leadership landscape, this issue is just as relevant. Leaders in various industries—from corporate executives to nonprofit directors—often struggle with the weight of responsibility, feeling as though they must control every detail. The fear of losing control or of tasks not being done "correctly" often prevents leaders from delegating. However, trying to do it all leads to burnout, inefficiency, and the stifling of organizational growth.

The Global Leadership Burden

Leaders around the world face this burden in different ways. In large corporations, executives may feel overwhelmed by the sheer volume of decisions they need to make, while in smaller organizations, leaders may struggle with limited resources and personnel. Across the globe, leaders in government, education, business, and beyond are increasingly expected to do more with less, leading to a growing sense of pressure and fatigue.

Jethro's wisdom offers a solution: instead of trying to do everything yourself, delegate responsibility to those who are capable and willing to lead alongside you. This not only lightens your load but also empowers others to contribute their talents and strengths.

The Importance of Empowering Others

At the core of Jethro's advice to Moses is the principle of empowerment. He told Moses to "select capable men from all the people—men who fear God, trustworthy men who hate dishonest gain—and appoint them as officials over thousands, hundreds, fifties, and tens" (Exodus 18:21). By doing this, Moses would create a system where leadership was shared, and people were given the opportunity to use their gifts and strengths to serve the community.

Empowering others is one of the most important aspects of relational leadership. When leaders delegate, they are not simply offloading tasks; they are giving people the opportunity to lead and grow. Empowerment fosters ownership, engagement, and motivation, as individuals feel valued and trusted.

In a global context, empowerment is even more critical. As organizations expand across borders, leaders must recognize the importance of delegating authority to local leaders who understand the cultural, social, and economic nuances of their regions. Global leaders who try to centralize control over every decision quickly find themselves overwhelmed and out of touch with local realities.

The Power of Trust

Effective delegation requires trust. Jethro instructed Moses to select trustworthy men—leaders who feared God and were committed to justice. Trust is the foundation of delegation. Leaders must be willing to trust others to make decisions, handle responsibilities, and take ownership of their roles.

Trust doesn't mean abandoning oversight; rather, it means creating a framework in which leaders can thrive and develop their own leadership skills. When leaders trust their teams, they foster an environment of accountability, creativity, and innovation.

Trust also plays a significant role in cross-cultural leadership. In global organizations, leaders must be able to trust local managers and team leaders to make decisions that are culturally and contextually appropriate. This requires building relationships of mutual respect and understanding, where local leaders are empowered to act in the best interests of their teams and the organization as a whole.

Building a Delegation Framework

Jethro's advice to Moses wasn't just about delegation in general; it was about creating a structured system of leadership. He advised Moses to appoint leaders over thousands, hundreds, fifties, and tens. This hierarchy allowed for efficient problem-solving, with only the most difficult cases reaching Moses.

In modern organizations, leaders must also create structured systems that facilitate effective delegation. Here are some key principles for building a delegation framework:

1. **Identify Capable Leaders:** Just as Jethro instructed Moses to select men who were capable and trustworthy, leaders today must identify individuals within their organizations who are equipped to handle leadership responsibilities. This involves recognizing their skills, character, and commitment.
2. **Clarify Roles and Responsibilities:** Effective delegation requires clear communication about expectations and boundaries. Leaders must clearly define the roles and responsibilities of those they delegate to, ensuring that everyone understands what is expected of them and how their role fits into the larger organizational goals.
3. **Provide Support and Resources:** Delegation is not simply handing off tasks and walking away. Leaders must ensure that those they delegate to have the resources, training, and support needed to succeed. This may include providing mentorship, tools, and access to information that will help them make informed decisions.
4. **Create a Hierarchy of Decision-Making:** Just as Moses was responsible for the most difficult cases, leaders today must create a system in which decisions are made at the appropriate levels. This allows for efficiency and prevents bottlenecks in decision-making.
5. **Foster Open Communication:** Delegation requires ongoing communication between leaders and those they delegate to. Leaders should encourage regular feedback, ask for updates, and be available for

consultation when needed. This ensures that the delegation process remains collaborative and effective.

The Benefits of Delegation and Empowerment

Delegation is not just about relieving the leader's workload; it has broader benefits for the organization as a whole. Empowering others to lead helps create a more dynamic, innovative, and resilient organization.

Here are some of the key benefits of delegation:

1. **Increased Efficiency**: When leaders delegate tasks to those who are capable and qualified, decision-making becomes more efficient. Teams can respond to issues more quickly, and leaders are free to focus on higher-level strategic decisions.
2. **Leadership Development**: Delegation provides opportunities for emerging leaders to develop their skills and gain experience. By empowering others to take on leadership roles, organizations create a pipeline of future leaders who are prepared to step up when needed.
3. **Enhanced Creativity and Innovation**: When people feel empowered to make decisions and take ownership of their roles, they are more likely to think creatively and propose innovative solutions. Delegation fosters a culture of collaboration, where diverse ideas and perspectives can thrive.
4. **Increased Morale and Engagement**: Employees who feel trusted and valued are more engaged in their work. Delegation sends a message that their contributions are important, which boosts morale and creates a sense of ownership and accountability.

5. **Global Adaptability**: In a global organization, delegation allows leaders to respond to the unique needs of different regions and markets. By empowering local leaders, global organizations can adapt more quickly to changing conditions and make decisions that are culturally appropriate.

Delegation in the Global Context

In today's globalized world, the principle of delegation is more important than ever. As organizations expand across borders, leaders must delegate authority to regional leaders who understand the specific cultural, economic, and political dynamics of their areas. This is not only practical but essential for success in a global context.

Global leaders must also navigate the complexities of cross-cultural leadership. Different cultures have different approaches to authority, hierarchy, and decision-making. Leaders who delegate must be aware of these cultural nuances and adapt their leadership style accordingly.

For example, in some cultures, delegation may be viewed as a sign of trust and empowerment, while in others, it may be seen as a leader shirking responsibility. Global leaders must be sensitive to these cultural differences and build relationships of trust and respect with their teams.

Conclusion: The Transformative Power of Delegation

Jethro's advice to Moses was more than just practical leadership guidance; it was a transformative moment that reshaped Moses' leadership style and allowed him to lead more effectively. By delegating responsibilities and empowering others, Moses was able to focus on the most critical aspects of his leadership while giving others the opportunity to grow and lead.

For modern leaders, the lesson is clear: trying to do everything yourself is not sustainable, and it limits the potential of your organization. Leadership thrives when leaders empower others, delegate responsibilities, and trust their teams to rise to the occasion.

In a global context, delegation is essential for navigating the complexities of cross-cultural leadership and adapting to the unique needs of different regions. Leaders who embrace delegation and empowerment create organizations that are more dynamic, resilient, and innovative.

As you continue your leadership journey, remember the wisdom of Jethro: "What you are doing is not good. You cannot handle it alone." The most effective leaders are those who recognize the power of empowering others and create structures that allow leadership to thrive at every level.

Delegation in a Global Context

In an increasingly globalized world, leaders often face complex challenges that require navigating diverse cultural, economic, and social landscapes. Each region, organization, or team may operate with its own set of norms, values, and expectations. As such, one-size-fits-all solutions rarely work effectively in leadership. To overcome this, delegation becomes not merely a tool but a necessity for success.

Through strategic delegation, leaders can entrust knowledgeable team members in various regions or departments with responsibilities that tap into their unique strengths and insights.

Delegation in cross-cultural leadership allows for a more tailored approach to management, giving room for regional and cultural expertise to shape decision-making. By trusting local leaders to manage operations within their context, organizations benefit from insights that a central leader may lack. Such delegation promotes a culture of respect and understanding, reinforcing the value of each individual's contributions to the organization's goals.

Empowerment for Organizational Dynamism, Resilience, and Innovation

When leaders delegate authority along with responsibility, they lay the groundwork for empowerment. Empowered team members are more likely to take ownership of their work, exercise creativity, and push boundaries in a constructive manner. This sense of autonomy fuels innovation because team members feel invested in the outcomes and are encouraged to approach challenges with fresh perspectives. Empowerment also leads to resilience, as a well-empowered team can adapt swiftly to unforeseen changes, leveraging collective wisdom and skills rather than waiting on centralized decisions.

Dynamic organizations continuously evolve with changing needs and market demands, and this adaptability is a direct outcome of distributed leadership. By empowering people across various organizational levels, leaders encourage agility, as multiple individuals contribute to problem-solving and decision-making. The empowered environment also fosters a stronger commitment, as people feel more accountable and enthusiastic about the role they play in the organization's success. This decentralized approach allows the organization to stay relevant and resilient in a rapidly changing world.

The Wisdom of Jethro: The Power of Shared Leadership

The counsel of Jethro to Moses, "What you are doing is not good. You cannot handle it alone," underscores an essential truth in leadership: even the most capable leaders cannot manage everything on their own. Jethro's advice highlights the dangers of a centralized, "one-man show" leadership style, where the weight of decision-making rests solely on one individual. Attempting to lead in isolation can lead to burnout, poor decision-making, and, ultimately, a less effective team.

In the biblical narrative, Jethro advised Moses to delegate his responsibilities, appointing capable people to manage smaller groups within the Israelite community. This decentralized leadership structure allowed Moses to focus on higher-level decision-making and prevented him from becoming overwhelmed. This wisdom remains relevant in modern leadership. Leaders who create structures that distribute responsibilities foster a culture where leadership can emerge at every level. Not only does this allow the organization to run more efficiently, but it also cultivates new leaders within the ranks.

Creating Structures for Sustainable Leadership

To allow leadership to thrive at every level, leaders must establish systems that encourage shared responsibility and continuous development. Such structures include mentorship programs, clear role definitions, and open communication channels. By setting up frameworks that facilitate collaboration and shared leadership, leaders can ensure that the organization is well-prepared to thrive, even in their absence.

Creating sustainable leadership structures also involves recognizing and nurturing potential in others. Effective leaders see the leadership qualities within their team members and actively seek to develop those skills. By investing in their growth, leaders cultivate a community where everyone is encouraged to lead, innovate, and contribute to the organization's vision.

Empowered Leadership: The Foundation of Lasting Success

The best leaders empower others to lead, recognizing that true strength comes from a collective effort. In contrast to command-and-control styles, relational and empowered leadership ensures that every member has a voice and a role in shaping the organization's future. As a leader, embracing the wisdom of Jethro means adopting a mindset of collaboration and a willingness to trust others with significant responsibility. This shift not only makes leadership more manageable but also establishes a legacy of resilience, innovation, and adaptability for the entire organization.

Ultimately, the most effective leaders are those who acknowledge that they cannot handle it alone. They empower others, create structures for shared leadership, and cultivate a culture where everyone can thrive. Leadership, in this sense, is not about doing everything but about facilitating an environment where everyone can contribute, grow, and lead. In this way, organizations become more dynamic, resilient, and innovative—prepared for any challenge that comes their way.

|Chapter 8|

Sustainable Leadership for a Global World

Exodus 18:13-16 – Leading with Wisdom and Balance

Leadership is often portrayed as a relentless pursuit of progress, success, and achievement. In many global contexts, leaders are expected to constantly drive forward, solving problems, meeting demands, and making decisions at a pace that leaves little room for rest or reflection. While this "always-on" mindset may seem necessary in today's fast-paced world, it can lead to burnout, inefficiency, and unsustainable leadership practices.

Moses found himself in such a situation in Exodus 18. From morning until evening, he sat before the people, handling every dispute and resolving every issue. His dedication to his role was unquestionable, but his approach was unsustainable. He was overwhelmed by the sheer volume of demands placed on him, and it was affecting both his effectiveness and the well-being of those he was leading. Jethro, his father-in-law, saw this and quickly pointed out the flaw in Moses' leadership style: "What you are doing is not good. You will surely wear yourself out, and these people with you" (Exodus 18:17-18).

Jethro's wisdom serves as a timeless lesson for leaders across the globe. In today's world, leaders must learn to lead with wisdom and balance. This chapter explores how sustainable leadership—rooted in strategic delegation, balance, and foresight—is essential for long-term success in the global leadership landscape.

The Danger of Unsustainable Leadership

Moses' situation is a familiar one for many modern leaders. As organizations grow, demands increase, and leaders often feel the pressure to take on more responsibilities. In an effort to meet the needs of their teams, organizations, or communities, they may overcommit, working long hours, handling every problem, and becoming involved in every decision. This approach, while well-intentioned, is ultimately unsustainable. Jethro's observation that Moses would "wear himself out" is a warning for leaders today. When leaders take on too much, they not only risk burnout but also create a bottleneck in decision-making. Their organizations become overly dependent on them, limiting the growth and development of other leaders. Moreover, overworked leaders may make poor decisions, lose sight of long-term strategy, and fail to nurture the relationships that are essential for effective leadership.

Global Leadership in a Complex World

In the global leadership context, the challenges of managing multiple demands are amplified. Leaders of multinational organizations must navigate different time zones, cultural expectations, legal systems, and market dynamics. The complexity of global leadership requires a different approach—one that balances short-term demands with long-term sustainability.

Unsustainable leadership is particularly dangerous in the global arena, where decisions have far-reaching consequences. Leaders who are constantly reactive, handling every issue as it arises, miss the opportunity to focus on strategic growth and long-term planning. Moreover, unsustainable leadership creates a ripple effect, leading to stressed and overworked teams, diminished innovation, and a culture of burnout.

Leading with Wisdom: Learning from Jethro's Counsel

The solution to Moses' unsustainable leadership style was found in Jethro's wise counsel. Jethro didn't just tell Moses to delegate tasks; he offered a framework for sustainable leadership that would allow Moses to lead effectively while preserving his well-being. This wisdom applies to leaders across all cultures and industries, offering practical lessons for sustainable leadership in today's global world.

1. The Wisdom of Prioritization

One of the first pieces of advice Jethro gave Moses was to focus on the most important matters. He instructed Moses to handle the most difficult cases while delegating smaller disputes to other capable leaders. This principle of prioritization is essential for modern leaders. In a world of constant demands and distractions, leaders must learn to identify the most critical tasks and focus their energy on them.

Prioritization in Global Leadership

In a global context, leaders must often balance competing priorities across different regions and markets. Effective global leaders are those who can identify the key areas where their attention is needed and delegate other responsibilities to local leaders. By focusing on strategic decisions and long-term vision, leaders can ensure that their organizations remain agile and responsive in a rapidly changing global environment.

Key strategies for Prioritization Include

- **Identifying Core Responsibilities:** Leaders must determine which tasks require their direct involvement and which can be delegated. This allows them to focus on the areas where their expertise and decision-making are most valuable.
- **Setting Clear Boundaries:** Leaders who prioritize well know when to say "no." They understand that taking on too many tasks dilutes their effectiveness and prevents them from focusing on what matters most.
- **Aligning Priorities with Strategic Goals:** Every leader faces numerous demands, but not all demands are of equal importance. Sustainable leadership requires aligning day-to-day tasks with long-term organizational goals. Leaders who keep their focus on the bigger picture are better equipped to make decisions that support the organization's overall mission.

2. The Wisdom of Delegation

Jethro's most practical advice to Moses was to appoint other leaders to share the burden of leadership. By delegating responsibilities to capable individuals, Moses could focus on the most pressing issues while empowering others to lead in their own capacities.

3. Delegation as a Sustainability Tool

Delegation is not just about reducing workload; it's about creating a leadership structure that is sustainable in the long term. Leaders who delegate empower others to develop their own leadership skills, contributing to the growth and resilience of the organization. Moreover, delegation allows leaders to focus on strategic decisions, fostering a culture of collaboration and trust.

In a global context, delegation is particularly important. Leaders of multinational organizations must delegate authority to regional leaders who understand the unique cultural, economic, and political dynamics of their regions. This not only lightens the load for global leaders but also ensures that decisions are made at the local level, where leaders are more attuned to the specific needs of their markets.

4. The Wisdom of Balance

One of the most important aspects of Jethro's advice was the emphasis on balance. He recognized that Moses' current approach was not only unsustainable for him personally but also for the people he was leading. "You will surely wear yourself out, and these people with you" (Exodus 18:18). Jethro's insight reminds leaders that balance is not just about personal well-being; it affects the entire organization.

Sustainable Leadership in a Global Context

The global leadership landscape presents unique challenges that require sustainable approaches. Leaders who operate across multiple regions, cultures, and time zones must balance the competing demands of their teams, markets, and stakeholders. Sustainable leadership in a global context involves:

1. **Cross-Cultural Sensitivity**: Leaders must be aware of the cultural dynamics that influence how teams operate in different parts of the world. Delegation, decision-making, and leadership styles can vary significantly across cultures. Sustainable leadership requires adapting to these cultural differences and building relationships based on mutual respect and understanding.
2. **Decentralized Leadership**: In global organizations, centralized decision-making can be inefficient and disconnected from local realities. Leaders must adopt a decentralized leadership model, empowering regional leaders to make decisions that reflect the unique needs of their markets.
3. **Technology-Enabled Collaboration**: Technology plays a critical role in enabling sustainable leadership in a global context. However, leaders must also recognize the limits of technology and ensure that personal relationships and trust are at the heart of global collaboration.

The Consequences of Unsustainable Leadership

The consequences of unsustainable leadership are far-reaching. Leaders who fail to prioritize, delegate, and balance their responsibilities not only risk personal burnout but also jeopardize the success of their organizations. Unsustainable leadership leads to:

Decision-Making Bottlenecks: When leaders try to manage every detail themselves, decisions are delayed, and innovation is stifled.

Burnout and Turnover: Overworked leaders and teams are more likely to experience burnout, leading to high turnover and decreased morale.

Short-Term Focus: Leaders who are constantly reactive are unable to focus on long-term strategy, leading to missed opportunities and a lack of direction.

By adopting sustainable leadership practices, leaders can avoid these pitfalls and create a culture of resilience, innovation, and collaboration.

Conclusion: Leading with Wisdom and Balance

Jethro's advice to Moses was not just about delegation; it was about creating a sustainable leadership model that allowed Moses to lead effectively without sacrificing his well-being or the well-being of those he served. This wisdom is just as relevant today as it was thousands of years ago.

Sustainable leadership is about more than just managing tasks; it's about leading with wisdom, balance, and foresight. In a global world where complexity and pressure are ever-increasing, leaders must adopt practices that ensure their leadership is sustainable in the long term. By prioritizing wisely, delegating effectively, and maintaining balance, leaders can create organizations that thrive in the present while building a foundation for future success.

The lesson from Moses and Jethro is clear: leadership is not a sprint but a marathon. Sustainable leadership is the key to not only surviving the race but finishing it strong.

Sustainable Leadership: Leading with Wisdom, Balance, and Foresight

In today's interconnected world, sustainable leadership goes beyond task management and efficiency; it requires a leader to cultivate a vision that encompasses the long-term health and growth of both people and the organization. This requires three key attributes: wisdom, balance, and foresight.

Wisdom: Learning from Experience and Leading with Insight

Wisdom in leadership is the ability to draw from past experiences, both successes and failures, to make informed and thoughtful decisions. In a global world, where rapid change is the norm, wisdom becomes the bedrock of sustainable leadership. It allows leaders to discern between short-term gains and long-term consequences, leading with a sense of purpose that is not swayed by immediate pressures or trends. Wise leaders know that their decisions ripple across time, impacting future leaders, teams, and organizational outcomes.

Moreover, wisdom in leadership involves a commitment to lifelong learning. Leaders who seek to grow intellectually, emotionally, and spiritually are more prepared to navigate challenges in a sustainable way. By embracing humility and a learning mindset, wise leaders create an environment where knowledge is valued and shared, fostering a culture of growth and resilience across the organization.

Balance: Managing Work, Health, and Relationships

Balance is essential to sustainable leadership, especially in a world where leaders are expected to do more with less and meet increasing demands. Without balance, leaders quickly succumb to burnout, which can compromise both their well-being and effectiveness. Sustainable leadership, therefore, involves setting boundaries, prioritizing personal health, and maintaining relationships outside of work.

Leaders who prioritize balance understand that their role is not only about achieving results but about creating a healthy, supportive environment for everyone. This includes fostering a work culture where employees feel encouraged to maintain their own work-life balance. By modeling balanced behavior, leaders send a powerful message to their teams: productivity and well-being are not mutually exclusive but are interdependent. Organizations that support this kind of environment are more likely to retain talent, as employees feel valued and respected as whole individuals, not just workers.

Foresight: Planning for the Future and Building Lasting Foundations

Foresight in leadership is the ability to anticipate future challenges and opportunities and to prepare for them proactively. In a global world marked by constant change, leaders who think ahead and make decisions with the future in mind build a foundation for sustainable success. This approach involves strategic planning, succession planning, and the flexibility to adapt to new circumstances.

Sustainable leaders cultivate foresight by involving others in the planning process. By drawing on the collective intelligence of their teams, they can identify emerging trends and challenges that may otherwise go unnoticed. Additionally, leaders with foresight focus on building a pipeline of future leaders within the organization. They understand that their legacy will be defined by the strength of those who come after them, and they actively invest in training, mentoring, and empowering the next generation.

The Lesson from Moses and Jethro: Leadership is a Marathon, Not a Sprint

The story of Moses and Jethro provides a powerful lesson in sustainable leadership. Moses, faced with the immense responsibility of leading the Israelite community, was at risk of burnout as he tried to handle every issue and decision himself. Jethro's advice—to delegate authority and allow others to share in leadership—emphasized the importance of sustainable practices in leadership.

In the same way, today's leaders are often tempted to do everything themselves, driven by a desire to achieve or a fear of relinquishing control. However, sustainable leadership requires acknowledging one's limits and embracing the power of shared leadership. By involving others, leaders not only lighten their load but also enable the growth and development of their team members.

Jethro's counsel reminds us that leadership is not a sprint, where the goal is to achieve as much as possible in a short time. Instead, it is a marathon—a long-term commitment to nurturing and guiding others while maintaining one's own strength and resilience. Sustainable leaders understand that they must pace themselves, prioritizing the long game over short-term achievements. In doing so, they ensure that their leadership impact extends beyond their immediate tenure, leaving a legacy of strength and endurance.

Practical Applications of Sustainable Leadership

1. **Effective Delegation**: Sustainable leaders recognize the importance of delegating responsibilities and empowering team members. This not only distributes the workload but also fosters a sense of ownership and accountability within the team. By delegating thoughtfully, leaders free themselves to focus on strategic matters and create opportunities for others to step into leadership roles.
2. **Prioritizing Self-Care and Well-Being**: Leaders who prioritize their own health set a positive example for their teams. Sustainable leadership includes practices such as taking regular breaks, setting boundaries, and seeking support when needed. By prioritizing self-care, leaders demonstrate that success is not worth sacrificing one's well-being, and they cultivate a more humane and supportive work culture.
3. **Building a Leadership Pipeline:** Sustainable leaders understand that their legacy will be shaped by the leaders who follow them. They invest in leadership development, mentoring, and providing growth opportunities for emerging leaders. This not only strengthens the organization but also ensures continuity and resilience in times of transition.
4. **Creating a Vision Aligned with Long-Term Goals**: A clear and compelling vision is essential for sustainable leadership. Leaders who articulate a vision that

extends beyond immediate goals inspire loyalty and commitment from their teams. This long-term perspective helps organizations weather short-term setbacks, as team members remain focused on the larger purpose that guides their efforts.

5. **Encouraging a Culture of Reflection and Learning** Sustainable leaders create environments where continuous learning and reflection are valued. They encourage their teams to learn from both successes and failures, promoting an attitude of growth and improvement. This reflective culture enhances resilience, as individuals and teams are better equipped to adapt and innovate in response to change.

In Summary: Sustainable Leadership for Lasting Success

Sustainable leadership in a global world requires wisdom, balance, and foresight. By embracing these qualities, leaders can guide their organizations through complexity, nurture a positive and balanced work environment, and prepare for future challenges. The lesson of Moses and Jethro underscores the importance of sharing leadership, recognizing that true success lies in the ability to lead in a way that sustains both the leader and those they serve.

Ultimately, sustainable leadership is the key to not only surviving but finishing strong. By adopting sustainable practices, leaders ensure that they—and their organizations—can thrive in the present while building a foundation for future success.

|Chapter 9|

Creating a Culture of Collaboration

Exodus 18:21–23 – Leadership through Teams

In today's globalized and interconnected world, the idea of a solitary leader, isolated from their team and making decisions in a vacuum, is not only outdated but also unsustainable. Effective leadership, especially in complex global environments, requires collaboration—working together across teams, departments, and regions to achieve common goals. This collaborative leadership model ensures that the collective strengths of the team are harnessed and that innovative solutions are fostered through shared ideas and mutual support.

In **Exodus 18:21–23**, Jethro's advice to Moses emphasized the importance of shared leadership. Jethro instructed Moses to appoint capable leaders who could manage smaller groups, distributing leadership responsibilities and allowing for better decision-making at different levels. This decentralized model of leadership created a structure in which collaboration and teamwork could thrive, ensuring that Moses was not burdened by every issue while empowering others to lead effectively.

This chapter will explore the importance of building a culture of collaboration in leadership and how modern leaders can apply this principle in diverse, global contexts. By fostering collaboration, leaders not only enhance organizational effectiveness but also cultivate an environment where innovation and trust flourish.

The Power of Collaboration in Leadership

Collaboration is the process of two or more people working together to achieve shared goals. In leadership, collaboration is crucial for several reasons:

1. **Increased Innovation:** When leaders foster a collaborative culture, they encourage the sharing of ideas and perspectives. This creates an environment where creativity thrives and innovative solutions are developed. People from different backgrounds and experiences bring unique insights, which can lead to breakthroughs that would not have been possible in a siloed environment.
2. **Efficient Problem-Solving:** No leader can solve every problem alone. Collaborative leadership ensures that issues are addressed by those closest to the problem, allowing for faster and more informed decision-making. By delegating responsibilities to others and trusting them to handle challenges, leaders can ensure that problems are solved efficiently and effectively.
3. **Stronger Relationships:** Collaboration fosters trust and mutual respect among team members. When leaders encourage collaboration, they create a sense of unity and shared purpose. This leads to stronger relationships within the team and a greater commitment to achieving common goals.
4. **Shared Accountability:** In a collaborative leadership model, accountability is shared across the team. This not only distributes responsibility but also empowers

team members to take ownership of their work and the organization's success.

Jethro's advice to Moses exemplified the importance of collaboration in leadership. By appointing leaders over groups of thousands, hundreds, fifties, and tens, Moses created a system of shared leadership that ensured efficiency, distributed decision-making, and reduced the burden on any one individual.

Building a Culture of Collaboration

Creating a culture of collaboration doesn't happen by accident. It requires intentional leadership practices, clear communication, and a commitment to fostering an environment where teamwork and mutual respect are valued. Here are some key strategies for building a culture of collaboration in leadership:

1. Break down Silos

Silos occur when teams or departments within an organization operate independently, with little communication or collaboration between them. This leads to inefficiencies, duplication of effort, and missed opportunities. Silos often develop when leaders fail to encourage cross-functional collaboration or when teams become too focused on their own goals.

To break down silos, leaders must:

- **Encourage Cross-Departmental Collaboration:** Leaders should actively promote collaboration between different teams and departments. This can be done through joint projects, cross-functional teams, or regular meetings where people from different areas of the organization come together to share ideas and updates.

- **Create a Shared Vision:** When everyone in the organization is working toward the same overarching goals, collaboration naturally follows. Leaders must ensure that the organization's mission and vision are clearly communicated and understood by all team members so they can align their efforts accordingly.
- **Foster Open Communication:** Collaboration thrives in an environment where communication is open and transparent. Leaders should encourage frequent and open communication between teams, providing the tools and platforms necessary for information sharing.

2. Empower Others to Lead

A key part of collaborative leadership is empowering others to lead. Jethro advised Moses to appoint capable leaders over different groups, giving them the authority to make decisions and resolve issues. By doing this, Moses not only reduced his own workload but also empowered others to take on leadership responsibilities.

Empowering others to lead is essential for fostering collaboration. When team members feel trusted and valued, they are more likely to take initiative and contribute their best ideas. To empower others, leaders should:

- **Delegate Responsibility:** Leaders must trust their teams to make decisions and take ownership of their work. By delegating authority, leaders give team members the opportunity to lead within their areas of expertise, contributing to the overall success of the organization.

- **Encourage Autonomy:** Collaborative cultures thrive when individuals have the autonomy to make decisions within their roles. Leaders should encourage autonomy while providing support and guidance when needed.
- **Recognize and Celebrate Contributions:** Empowering others also means recognizing their contributions and celebrating their successes. Leaders should acknowledge the achievements of their teams and publicly celebrate collaborative efforts.

3. Leverage Technology for Global Collaboration

In today's global world, collaboration often takes place across borders, time zones, and cultures. Advances in technology have made it easier than ever for teams to collaborate, even when they are not physically in the same location. Leaders must leverage technology to foster collaboration in global organizations.

Key technologies that enable global collaboration include:

- **Video Conferencing Tools:** Platforms like Zoom, Microsoft Teams, and Google Meet allow teams to meet face-to-face, regardless of location. Leaders should encourage regular video meetings to maintain personal connections and foster collaboration across global teams.
- **Project Management Tools:** Tools like Asana, Trello, and Monday.com help teams stay organized, manage tasks, and collaborate on projects. Leaders should

implement these tools to ensure that team members are aligned and working toward shared goals.

- **Collaboration Platforms:** Platforms like Slack or Microsoft Teams offer spaces where teams can communicate, share documents, and collaborate in real time. Leaders should encourage the use of these platforms to facilitate open communication and information sharing.

By leveraging these technologies, leaders can create an environment where collaboration is seamless, even across global teams.

Collaboration in Cross-Cultural Leadership

In a global context, collaboration takes on additional complexity. Leaders must navigate cultural differences in communication styles, decision-making processes, and leadership expectations. Understanding these cultural nuances is critical for fostering effective collaboration across diverse teams.

1. Understanding Cultural Differences

Cultural differences can impact how teams collaborate and how leadership is perceived. For example, in some cultures, a hierarchical leadership structure is the norm, while in others, a more egalitarian approach is preferred. Leaders must be sensitive to these differences and adapt their leadership style accordingly.

To foster collaboration in cross-cultural environments, leaders should:

Promote Cultural Awareness: Leaders must educate themselves and their teams about the cultural backgrounds of their colleagues. This can be done through cultural training, open discussions, and promoting an inclusive environment where diverse perspectives are valued.

Adapt Communication Styles: Communication is key to collaboration, but different cultures have different communication styles. Leaders should be mindful of these differences and adapt their communication to ensure clarity and respect. For example, some cultures may prefer direct communication, while others may value more indirect or nuanced conversations.

Encourage Cross-Cultural Team Building: Leaders can foster cross-cultural collaboration by creating opportunities for team building across regions. This could include international retreats, cross-cultural exchanges, or virtual team-building activities that bring diverse teams together.

Building Trust across Cultures

Trust is the foundation of collaboration, but trust-building can vary across cultures. In some cultures, trust is built quickly through competence and results, while in others, trust is built slowly through personal relationships and shared experiences. Leaders must understand how trust is built in different cultural contexts and take steps to foster it.

To build trust across cultures, leaders should:

Invest in Relationships: In cultures where personal relationships are key to building trust, leaders should take the time to get to know their team members on a personal level. This could involve informal meetings, social events, or one-on-one conversations.

Be Consistent and Transparent: Trust is also built through consistency and transparency. Leaders should be clear about expectations, follow through on commitments, and provide transparent communication about organizational goals and decisions.

Respect Cultural Norms: Leaders should demonstrate respect for cultural norms and practices, acknowledging and honoring the values of different cultures within the organization. This respect fosters mutual trust and collaboration across diverse teams.

The Role of the Leader in Collaborative Teams

While collaboration is a team effort, the leader plays a critical role in setting the tone for collaboration. Leaders must actively foster a collaborative culture by modeling collaborative behaviors, setting expectations for teamwork, and creating an environment where collaboration is encouraged and rewarded.

1. Model Collaborative Behaviors

Leaders set the example for their teams. If leaders want their teams to collaborate, they must model collaborative behaviors themselves. This means being open to input from others, seeking out diverse perspectives, and working alongside the team to achieve shared goals.

2. Create a Safe Environment for Collaboration

Collaboration requires a safe environment where team members feel comfortable sharing their ideas, even if they are unconventional or outside the norm. Leaders must create a culture of psychological safety, where individuals feel free to contribute without fear of criticism or retribution.

3. Encourage and Reward Collaboration

Leaders should actively encourage collaboration by recognizing and rewarding collaborative efforts. This could involve celebrating team achievements, providing incentives for cross-functional projects, or offering formal recognition for individuals who exemplify collaborative leadership.

Conclusion: Leading Through Collaboration

In Exodus 18, Jethro's advice to Moses not only provided a practical solution to leadership fatigue but also laid the foundation for a collaborative leadership model. By appointing leaders over different groups, Moses created a system where leadership was shared, decisions were made at different levels, and collaboration was prioritized.

For modern leaders, the lesson is clear: leadership thrives when it is shared. By fostering a culture of collaboration, leaders can harness the collective strengths of their teams, encourage innovation, and build stronger relationships. In a globalized world, collaboration is more important than ever. Leaders who prioritize collaboration—both within their teams and across cultural boundaries—are better equipped to lead effectively in a rapidly changing world.

Creating a Culture of Collaboration: The Foundation of Shared Leadership

In a world that is more interconnected than ever, the challenges facing leaders are rarely solved by individual effort alone. The complexities of today's global landscape require leaders to adopt a collaborative mindset, one that values the strengths, perspectives, and ideas of every team member. By fostering a culture of collaboration, leaders not only optimize the talents within their teams but also create a foundation for sustainable success. Collaborative leadership encourages shared responsibility, reduces silos, and empowers people at every level to contribute to the organization's mission.

Collaboration isn't merely about assigning tasks and expecting individuals to work together; it's about creating an environment where people feel free to share their ideas, express differing perspectives, and leverage collective intelligence. A true culture of collaboration is built on trust, open communication, and shared goals. When these elements are in place, collaboration transforms from a strategy to a deeply ingrained cultural value that drives innovation, resilience, and growth.

Harnessing Collective Strengths and Diversity

A collaborative culture enables leaders to harness the unique strengths of each team member. People bring different skills, experiences, and perspectives to the table, and collaboration allows these differences to enrich the organization's approach to problem-solving. Instead of relying solely on the ideas of a single leader, a collaborative environment encourages every team member to contribute their expertise, which can result in more comprehensive, creative solutions.

In a globalized world, teams often consist of individuals from various backgrounds, cultures, and disciplines. This diversity can be a powerful asset if leaders cultivate a culture that values each individual's contributions. Diverse perspectives often lead to breakthroughs in innovation because they bring fresh insights and approaches that might not be considered otherwise. By leveraging the collective strengths of a diverse team, collaborative leaders make more well-rounded, adaptable, and innovative decisions.

Encouraging Innovation through Collaboration

Innovation thrives in collaborative environments where people feel safe to take risks and share unconventional ideas. In a culture of collaboration, team members know that their contributions will be valued and respected, which fosters an atmosphere of trust and psychological safety. This environment is crucial for innovation because it encourages team members to think beyond traditional solutions, try new approaches, and learn from failures.

Collaboration also accelerates the process of innovation by enabling the rapid exchange of ideas. When people work together, they can build on each other's insights, refining ideas through feedback and constructive critique. Leaders who encourage this kind of collaboration position their teams to move faster, stay agile, and remain competitive in a rapidly changing market.

Building Stronger Relationships and Reducing Silos

A collaborative culture strengthens relationships across the organization. When people work closely together toward shared goals, they develop trust and mutual respect. These strong relationships form the backbone of a resilient team that can withstand challenges and adapt to changes. Collaboration breaks down silos, bridging gaps between departments, teams, or regions. In large or global organizations, silos can become significant barriers to effective communication and alignment. By prioritizing collaboration, leaders encourage cross-functional interaction, which enhances coordination and promotes unity within the organization.

Leaders who actively work to reduce silos promote a sense of belonging and cohesion. In a collaborative culture, everyone feels connected to the organization's mission and vision, regardless of their specific role. This unity leads to higher morale, as team members feel they are part of a collective effort rather than isolated units working in parallel.

Collaborating across Cultural Boundaries in a Globalized World

In a global context, collaboration extends beyond an organization's internal structure. Effective leaders understand that partnerships with stakeholders from different cultural backgrounds can be invaluable sources of growth and insight. By embracing collaboration across cultural boundaries, leaders demonstrate cultural humility, a willingness to learn from others, and an openness to diverse perspectives.

Global collaboration can be challenging due to differences in language, customs, and communication styles. Leaders who are adept at fostering cross-cultural collaboration invest in cultural competence training, encourage open dialogue about differences, and set up structures to facilitate understanding. By prioritizing collaboration across borders, leaders not only enhance their organization's global reach but also increase its adaptability, as team members become more adept at navigating various cultural contexts.

Key Elements for Fostering a Culture of Collaboration

1. **Establishing Shared Goals and Purpose**: Collaboration is most effective when everyone is working toward a common objective. Leaders should articulate a clear vision and set shared goals that unite the team. When team members understand the larger purpose, they are more likely to collaborate willingly and enthusiastically.
2. **Promoting Open Communication**: Open, transparent communication is essential for collaboration. Leaders should encourage team members to express their ideas, concerns, and insights freely. Regular check-ins, brainstorming sessions, and cross-functional meetings create spaces where information flows freely and people can share their perspectives.
3. **Building Trust and Psychological Safety**: Trust is the foundation of collaboration. Leaders must foster a climate where team members feel safe to take risks, speak up, and even make mistakes without fear of reprisal. This psychological safety empowers people to engage fully and contribute their best work.
4. **Encouraging Diverse Perspectives and Inclusive Participation**: Leaders who value diversity invite

multiple perspectives, creating a more inclusive environment. This means actively encouraging contributions from everyone, including those who may typically be less vocal. Inclusivity in collaboration strengthens the team's ability to innovate and adapt to change.

5. **Empowering Team Members with Autonomy**: Collaborative cultures thrive when team members are empowered to make decisions within their areas of responsibility. Leaders who trust their team members and give them autonomy create a more engaged and proactive workforce. Empowerment also helps prevent bottlenecks, as team members feel confident in taking initiative.
6. **Providing Resources and Support for Collaborative Tools**: Collaboration in a modern, often remote world is supported by digital tools and platforms that enable seamless interaction. Leaders should invest in the necessary technology and provide training to ensure that team members can communicate and collaborate effectively, no matter where they are located.

The Lasting Impact of Collaborative Leadership

Leaders who foster a culture of collaboration create organizations that are not only more innovative and resilient but also more enjoyable places to work. Collaboration instills a sense of ownership and pride, as team members feel they are contributing to something meaningful. Collaborative organizations also tend to experience higher levels of employee satisfaction and retention, as people feel valued and supported in their roles.

Moreover, a collaborative culture equips organizations to respond effectively to complex global challenges. Leaders who prioritize collaboration across cultural boundaries make their teams more adaptable, better prepared for international growth, and more sensitive to the needs of diverse stakeholders.

In Summary: Leadership Thrives When It Is Shared

In an era where no single leader or department has all the answers, collaboration has become the cornerstone of effective leadership. Leaders who cultivate a collaborative culture position their teams to leverage collective strengths, encourage innovation, and build stronger, more resilient relationships. As the world becomes increasingly globalized, collaboration within and across cultural boundaries becomes even more crucial.

By prioritizing collaboration, modern leaders not only meet the demands of a rapidly changing world but also create organizations that are adaptable, united, and prepared for the future. Leadership, ultimately, thrives when it is shared—when everyone is invited to contribute, learn, and grow together. This collaborative spirit is the essence of sustainable, impactful leadership in the modern age.

|Chapter 10|

Emotional Intelligence – The Relational Leader's Secret Weapon

Exodus 18:23 – Leading with Empathy and Understanding

In the modern world of leadership, where diverse teams and complex dynamics are the norm, emotional intelligence (EQ) has emerged as a key component of effective leadership. While technical skills, strategic thinking, and decision-making are critical, a leader's ability to understand and manage their own emotions, as well as the emotions of others, can make the difference between success and failure. The concept of emotional intelligence is about more than just being "nice" or understanding feelings—it's about using emotional awareness to build stronger relationships, resolve conflicts, inspire others, and lead with empathy.

Jethro's counsel to Moses in Exodus 18 serves as an early example of relational leadership grounded in emotional intelligence. Jethro's advice was not just practical; it was rooted in a deep understanding of human nature, empathy for Moses' situation, and a desire to ensure that both Moses and the people were cared for. Emotional intelligence enabled Jethro to offer wise counsel that helped Moses lead more effectively while maintaining his emotional and physical well-being.

This chapter will explore how emotional intelligence plays a vital role in relational leadership and how leaders across the globe can develop and leverage this crucial skill to lead with empathy, build trust, and create a more resilient and cohesive team.

The Components of Emotional Intelligence

Emotional intelligence is often broken down into five core components: self-awareness, self-regulation, motivation, empathy, and social skills. Each of these components plays a critical role in a leader's ability to connect with others, navigate complex interpersonal dynamics, and lead with confidence and compassion.

1. Self-Awareness

Self-awareness is the foundation of emotional intelligence. It involves understanding your own emotions, strengths, weaknesses, values, and impact on others. Leaders who are self-aware are better able to manage their reactions, make informed decisions, and lead with authenticity.

In the case of Moses, self-awareness was key to recognizing that his leadership style was unsustainable. It was Jethro's observation and intervention that highlighted the need for Moses to reflect on his limitations. Self-aware leaders, like Moses, are open to feedback and willing to adjust their behavior to improve their effectiveness.

Developing Self-Awareness

To cultivate self-awareness, leaders must take time for self-reflection, seek feedback from trusted colleagues, and be honest about their strengths and areas for growth. Tools such as personality assessments, journaling, and mindfulness practices can also help leaders develop a deeper understanding of themselves.

2. Self-Regulation

Self-regulation refers to the ability to manage one's emotions and impulses. Leaders who can self-regulate are able to stay calm under pressure, control their reactions, and respond to challenges with composure. This is essential for maintaining a positive and productive work environment.

In Exodus 18, Moses' initial reaction to Jethro's advice was one of openness rather than defensiveness. His ability to self-regulate allowed him to listen without becoming overwhelmed or reacting negatively. Leaders who can regulate their emotions are better equipped to handle criticism, resolve conflicts, and make thoughtful decisions.

Practicing Self-Regulation

Leaders can develop self-regulation by practicing mindfulness, managing stress through healthy habits, and pausing before reacting in emotionally charged situations. The ability to take a step back, assess the situation, and respond calmly is a hallmark of emotionally intelligent leadership.

3. Motivation

Motivation, in the context of emotional intelligence, refers to the drive to achieve goals for reasons beyond external rewards. Motivated leaders are passionate about their work, driven by a sense of purpose, and committed to personal and organizational growth. This intrinsic motivation inspires others and fosters a culture of excellence.

Moses was motivated by his calling to lead the Israelites, but his ability to sustain that motivation depended on adopting a leadership structure that was sustainable. Leaders with high emotional intelligence are not only motivated themselves but also know how to inspire and motivate their teams.

Fostering Motivation

Leaders can foster motivation by aligning their work with a sense of purpose, setting clear and achievable goals, and celebrating progress along the way. A motivated leader inspires others to take ownership of their work and strive for excellence.

4. Empathy

Empathy is the ability to understand and share the feelings of others. It is one of the most critical aspects of emotional intelligence because it allows leaders to connect with their team members on a deeper level, understand their needs, and respond with compassion. Empathy builds trust, fosters collaboration, and enhances team morale.

Jethro's advice to Moses was rooted in empathy. He recognized that Moses was overwhelmed and exhausted, and he sought to alleviate that burden by offering a practical solution. Empathetic leaders, like Jethro, are attuned to the emotional state of their team members and are proactive in addressing their needs.

Developing Empathy

Leaders can develop empathy by actively listening to others, seeking to understand their perspectives, and responding with compassion. This involves putting oneself in another person's shoes and being sensitive to their emotions and experiences. Regular check-ins with team members, open communication, and creating a safe space for emotional expression are all ways to foster empathy in leadership.

5. Social Skills

Social skills refer to the ability to manage relationships effectively, communicate clearly, and build networks of support. Leaders with strong social skills can influence others, resolve conflicts, and foster collaboration. They are skilled at managing teams, navigating complex interpersonal dynamics, and creating a positive work environment.

In Exodus 18, Moses demonstrated strong social skills by listening to Jethro's advice, communicating his vision clearly to his appointed leaders, and fostering a collaborative leadership structure. Socially skilled leaders can bring people together, build consensus, and inspire collective action.

Enhancing Social Skills

Leaders can enhance their social skills by improving their communication abilities, practicing conflict resolution techniques, and actively building relationships within and outside their teams. Building rapport, fostering teamwork, and being approachable are key aspects of developing strong social skills.

The Role of Emotional Intelligence in Global Leadership

In a global leadership context, emotional intelligence is even more critical. Leaders who work across cultures, time zones, and geographies must navigate a diverse range of emotional and interpersonal dynamics. Emotional intelligence enables leaders to connect with people from different cultural backgrounds, understand their unique challenges, and foster collaboration across boundaries.

1. Cross-Cultural Empathy

Empathy becomes particularly important in global leadership, where leaders must work with individuals from diverse cultural backgrounds. Cultural differences can influence how emotions are expressed, how conflict is managed, and how leadership is perceived. Emotionally intelligent leaders are sensitive to these cultural nuances and adapt their leadership style accordingly.

For example, in some cultures, open emotional expression is encouraged, while in others, it may be seen as inappropriate. Leaders with high emotional intelligence recognize these differences and respond in ways that are culturally appropriate, building trust and fostering effective collaboration.

2. Managing Remote Teams with Emotional Intelligence

In today's global economy, many leaders manage remote or distributed teams. Emotional intelligence plays a key role in managing remote teams, as leaders must find ways to build relationships and foster trust despite physical distance. Leaders with high emotional intelligence prioritize communication, ensure that team members feel connected and supported, and create opportunities for remote employees to engage with their colleagues. This may include virtual check-ins, team-building activities, and ensuring that remote workers have the resources they need to succeed.

3. Emotional Intelligence in Crisis Leadership Global leaders often face crises, whether they are economic, environmental, or health-related. Leaders with high emotional intelligence are better equipped to navigate crises by managing their own emotions, responding with empathy to the concerns of their teams, and making decisions that balance emotional and practical considerations.

   During crises, emotionally intelligent leaders demonstrate resilience and provide a steady, reassuring presence. They are able to acknowledge the emotional toll of the crisis on their teams while maintaining a focus on solutions and moving forward.

The Impact of Emotional Intelligence on Team Performance Emotional intelligence doesn't just benefit the leader; it has a profound impact on team performance as well. Teams led by emotionally intelligent leaders tend to be more engaged, productive, and cohesive. Here's how emotional intelligence influences team dynamics:

1. **Improved Communication:** Emotionally intelligent leaders foster open and transparent communication within their teams. They encourage team members to express their thoughts and feelings, which leads to greater understanding and fewer misunderstandings. Open communication also helps to resolve conflicts before they escalate, creating a more harmonious work environment.

2. **Increased Trust:** Trust is the foundation of any successful team, and emotionally intelligent leaders are skilled at building and maintaining trust. By demonstrating empathy, transparency, and reliability, leaders create an environment where team members feel safe and valued. This trust leads to greater collaboration, innovation, and accountability.
3. **Higher Engagement:** Teams that feel supported emotionally are more engaged in their work. Emotionally intelligent leaders recognize the emotional needs of their team members and provide the encouragement, recognition, and support needed to keep morale high. This leads to greater job satisfaction and higher levels of productivity.

Developing Emotional Intelligence in Leadership

Emotional intelligence is not an innate trait; it can be developed and strengthened over time. Leaders who want to enhance their emotional intelligence can do so through intentional practice, reflection, and feedback.

Here are some strategies for developing emotional intelligence:

- **Seek Feedback**: Regularly ask for feedback from colleagues, team members, and mentors to gain insight into how your emotions and behavior are perceived. Use this feedback to make adjustments and improve your emotional awareness.
- **Practice Mindfulness**: Mindfulness exercises, such as meditation and deep breathing, can help leaders develop greater self-awareness and self-regulation. By

becoming more attuned to their emotions, leaders can respond to challenges with greater calm and clarity.

- **Develop Empathy**: Actively practice empathy by listening to others without judgment, seeking to understand their perspectives, and responding with compassion. This can be done through regular check-ins, one-on-one meetings, and creating a culture where emotional expression is valued.
- **Enhance Communication Skills**: Work on improving your communication skills by practicing active listening, asking open-ended questions, and being clear and transparent in your messaging. Strong communication is essential for building emotional intelligence.

Conclusion: Leading with Emotional Intelligence

Emotional intelligence is not just a "soft skill"—it's a critical component of effective leadership, especially in today's global, fast-paced, and complex environment. Leaders who develop and leverage their emotional intelligence are better equipped to build strong relationships, manage conflicts, inspire their teams, and navigate the emotional challenges of leadership. Jethro's advice to Moses in Exodus 18 highlights the importance of emotional intelligence in leadership. By leading with empathy, understanding the emotional dynamics of the people he led, and implementing a collaborative leadership structure, Moses was able to create a more sustainable and effective leadership model.

For modern leaders, emotional intelligence is the secret weapon that enables them to lead with authenticity, compassion, and resilience. By developing self-awareness, self-regulation, empathy, and social skills, leaders can foster stronger relationships, enhance team performance, and create a culture of trust and collaboration.

Emotional Intelligence: More than a "Soft Skill" in Leadership

Emotional intelligence (EI) refers to the ability to recognize, understand, manage, and use one's emotions constructively, as well as to relate empathetically to the emotions of others. While it's often considered a "soft skill," EI is a foundational skill for relational leaders, especially in a fast-paced, globalized world where leaders face an array of emotional and interpersonal challenges. Unlike technical skills or industry knowledge, EI allows leaders to navigate the human aspects of leadership with authenticity and adaptability.
In an era where change is constant and relationships are central to success, leaders with high EI are better positioned to inspire trust, manage conflicts, and motivate teams. They understand that leadership is not merely about tasks or targets but about understanding and guiding people. This capacity makes EI a true "secret weapon" for relational leaders, enabling them to approach leadership with empathy, intuition, and insight.

The Four Pillars of Emotional Intelligence in Leadership

1. **Self-Awareness:** Self-awareness is the foundation of EI. Leaders who are self-aware understand their own emotions, strengths, weaknesses, and triggers. They recognize how their feelings influence their thoughts, behaviors, and decisions. In leadership, self-awareness

allows a leader to identify and control their reactions, even in high-stress situations, which promotes stability and predictability—qualities that are highly valued by teams.

Self-aware leaders also know when to step back and reassess their approaches, allowing them to model humility and a growth mindset. They are open to feedback and continually seek to improve themselves. This transparency and self-knowledge set the stage for authentic leadership, as teams are more likely to respect and trust leaders who demonstrate honesty about their own strengths and areas for growth.

2. **Self-Regulation**: Self-regulation is the ability to control one's emotional responses, particularly under pressure or in challenging situations. Leaders with high self-regulation manage their emotions rather than being managed by them. They don't react impulsively or allow negative emotions to influence their decisions. This ability to remain calm, thoughtful, and consistent in the face of adversity creates a stable environment for teams, fostering a sense of security and trust. Self-regulation also helps leaders to respond to conflicts with a constructive mindset. Instead of letting emotions drive a wedge between them and their team, emotionally intelligent leaders address issues diplomatically and work towards resolution. This approach reduces friction, promotes harmony, and maintains focus on shared goals.
3. **Empathy**: Empathy is the capacity to understand and feel the emotions of others. It is an essential skill for relational leaders because it allows them to connect

deeply with their teams, recognize individual needs, and respond compassionately to challenges. In today's globalized world, empathy is especially valuable, as leaders often work with people from diverse cultural backgrounds. An empathetic leader understands and respects these differences, fostering an inclusive and respectful work environment.

Empathy in leadership goes beyond simply acknowledging others' emotions—it involves actively supporting team members in meaningful ways. For example, an empathetic leader might recognize when a team member is struggling with a personal issue and offer flexibility or additional resources. This type of compassionate support strengthens the bond between leaders and their teams, boosting morale, engagement, and loyalty.

4. **Social Skills:** Social skills encompass a range of interpersonal abilities that enable leaders to communicate effectively, build networks, resolve conflicts, and inspire others. Leaders with strong social skills can articulate their vision clearly, motivate teams with ease, and build a culture of collaboration and trust. Social skills allow leaders to facilitate open communication, actively listen to feedback, and encourage participation.

Effective social skills are particularly crucial in conflict resolution. Leaders who are skilled at managing relationships can mediate conflicts, foster understanding, and find common ground. This capability promotes unity and resilience within teams, as individuals feel heard, valued, and motivated to work toward shared goals.

The Role of Emotional Intelligence in Effective Leadership

1. **Building Strong Relationships**: Emotional intelligence enables leaders to build genuine, trusting relationships with their teams. When leaders are self-aware, empathetic, and capable of regulating their emotions, they create a foundation of trust and respect. Teams feel comfortable approaching emotionally intelligent leaders, as they know these leaders will respond with fairness and understanding. Strong relationships are the backbone of any effective team, as they promote collaboration, reduce misunderstandings, and enhance loyalty.
2. **Managing Conflicts**: Conflict is inevitable in any organization, but emotionally intelligent leaders approach it constructively. By using empathy and social skills, leaders can address the underlying emotional dynamics in conflicts and work toward solutions that respect everyone's perspectives. Instead of allowing tensions to disrupt the team, leaders who leverage their emotional intelligence can turn conflicts into opportunities for growth, understanding, and unity.
3. **Inspiring Teams**: Leaders with high emotional intelligence are often more effective at inspiring their teams, as they connect with people on a personal level. They understand what motivates each team member and can tailor their approach to inspire action. Leaders who empathize with their teams' aspirations and struggles are better able to motivate them authentically, as they address both professional goals

and personal well-being. This connection fosters a shared sense of purpose and motivates teams to excel.

4. **Navigating the Emotional Challenges of Leadership**: Leadership is often emotionally demanding, requiring resilience, composure, and courage. Emotionally intelligent leaders are better equipped to handle these challenges because they understand and manage their emotions effectively. By remaining calm and composed, they serve as role models for their teams, showing that challenges can be faced with a positive attitude and a proactive mindset. This resilience is essential for sustainable leadership, as it helps leaders avoid burnout and maintain their effectiveness over the long term.

Jethro's Advice to Moses: Emotional Intelligence in Action

The counsel of Jethro to Moses in Exodus 18 is a powerful illustration of emotional intelligence in leadership. Jethro, observing Moses' approach to leadership, noticed that he was taking on too much and neglecting the emotional and relational needs of both himself and his people. Jethro's advice—to appoint other capable leaders to share the responsibility—reflects a profound understanding of empathy, self-regulation, and delegation.

Through Jethro's counsel, Moses was able to create a more sustainable and emotionally balanced leadership structure. By involving others and leading with empathy, Moses could better meet the needs of his people and create a collaborative model that allowed for growth and resilience. This story highlights the importance of recognizing emotional dynamics in leadership and the power of collaborative structures that value and empower others.

Developing Emotional Intelligence as a Leader

To harness emotional intelligence effectively, leaders must actively cultivate it through continuous practice and self-reflection:

- **Practice Self-Reflection:** Taking time to reflect on one's emotions, reactions, and motivations helps build self-awareness. Leaders who are mindful of their internal states are better equipped to manage them.
- **Seek Feedback:** Emotional intelligence can be developed by seeking honest feedback from peers and team members. Feedback offers valuable insights into how others perceive a leader's actions and provides a foundation for growth.
- **Engage in Empathy-Building Activities:** Leaders can practice empathy by taking the time to understand each team member's perspective. Listening actively, asking open-ended questions, and demonstrating understanding can strengthen empathy over time.
- **Develop Conflict-Resolution Skills:** Since emotionally intelligent leaders are adept at managing conflicts, they can benefit from training in conflict resolution, active listening, and negotiation. These skills help leaders address issues with a constructive mindset.

Emotional Intelligence: The Key to Authentic, Compassionate, and Resilient Leadership. In a world that is increasingly dynamic and diverse, emotional intelligence is indispensable for leaders who aspire to lead effectively and sustainably. The ability to connect authentically, manage emotions constructively, and approach relationships with empathy and respect is what sets emotionally intelligent leaders apart.

For modern leaders, emotional intelligence is indeed a "secret weapon" that enables them to lead with authenticity, compassion, and resilience. By cultivating self-awareness, self-regulation, empathy, and social skills, leaders can build stronger relationships, enhance team performance, and foster a culture of trust and collaboration. Emotional intelligence not only equips leaders to handle the relational challenges of leadership but also positions them to leave a lasting, positive impact on their organizations and the people they lead.

|Chapter 11|

Longevity in Leadership – Sustaining Influence through Relationships

Exodus 18:24-27 – Leadership That Endures

One of the hallmarks of great leadership is longevity—the ability to maintain influence, effectiveness, and impact over time. Leadership is not just about the moment; it's about the legacy that leaders leave behind. Sustaining influence requires more than skill or strategy; it demands that leaders build strong, lasting relationships, foster trust, and create a foundation that supports future leaders.

In Exodus 18:24-27, Moses followed Jethro's advice, implementing a leadership structure that allowed him to delegate responsibilities and empower others to lead. This shift not only lightened Moses' burden but also created a sustainable model of leadership that would last beyond his individual capacity. Moses' leadership endured because it was built on relationships—relationships with God, with his people, and with the leaders he appointed to share the load.

This chapter explores the principles of relational leadership that contribute to longevity, offering insights on how modern leaders can sustain their influence over time, mentor future leaders, and create a lasting legacy.

The Importance of Sustainable Leadership

Sustainable leadership is not about working harder or taking on more responsibilities; it's about building a leadership model that endures through strong relationships, delegation, and empowerment. Many leaders burn out because they try to do too much on their own. The key to longevity is recognizing the importance of building a leadership team, empowering others, and creating a culture where leadership is shared.

Moses' initial approach to leadership was unsustainable. He took on the full responsibility of leading the Israelites, managing disputes, and resolving every issue. This left him exhausted and unable to focus on the most critical aspects of his role. Jethro's advice to delegate authority and appoint capable leaders over smaller groups was not only a practical solution but also a model for sustainable leadership that ensured the long-term success of Moses' mission.

Sustainable Leadership in a Global Context

In today's global environment, the pressures of leadership are amplified. Leaders are expected to navigate complex challenges, drive innovation, and manage diverse teams, all while maintaining a high level of personal performance. The demands of global leadership can quickly become overwhelming without a sustainable leadership approach.

Sustainable leadership involves building strong relationships with key stakeholders, empowering teams to take ownership of their roles, and creating systems that allow the organization to thrive without the constant oversight of a single leader. This approach not only ensures the longevity of the leader but also the long-term success of the organization.

Building Relationships That Last

At the heart of sustainable leadership is the ability to build and maintain strong relationships. These relationships form the foundation of a leader's influence and are key to ensuring that leadership endures beyond any one individual.

1. **Trust and Respect**: Trust and respect are the cornerstones of any lasting relationship. Leaders who build trust with their teams, colleagues, and stakeholders create an environment where people feel valued and motivated to contribute their best. Trust is earned through consistency, integrity, and transparency.

Leaders like Moses gained the trust of their people by demonstrating that they had their best interests at heart. Moses' willingness to delegate authority and empower others to lead showed that he trusted his appointed leaders, and in turn, they trusted him to guide them wisely.

Building Trust

To build trust as a leader, it's important to:

- **Be Transparent:** Share information openly and honestly with your team. Transparency fosters trust by showing that you have nothing to hide and that you value open communication.
- **Follow Through on Commitments:** Consistency is key to building trust. Leaders who make promises and follow through on them demonstrate reliability and build a foundation of trust with their teams.
- **Show Respect:** Treat others with respect, regardless of their position or role within the organization. Leaders

who respect their team members create a culture of mutual respect and collaboration.

2. **Mentorship and Succession Planning**: Longevity in leadership requires a commitment to developing future leaders. Moses' decision to appoint leaders over groups of thousands, hundreds, fifties, and tens was an early example of succession planning. By mentoring and empowering these leaders, Moses ensured that the leadership structure would endure even in his absence.

Mentorship is a key part of sustaining influence. Leaders who invest in the development of others create a ripple effect, passing on their knowledge, values, and skills to the next generation of leaders. This not only strengthens the organization but also solidifies the leader's legacy.

Developing Future Leaders

To develop future leaders and ensure a smooth leadership transition, leaders should:

- **Identify High-Potential Individuals:** Look for individuals who demonstrate leadership potential, a strong work ethic, and a commitment to the organization's values. These are the people who will become the next generation of leaders.
- **Provide Opportunities for Growth:** Give emerging leaders the opportunity to take on new responsibilities, lead projects, and make decisions. This helps them develop the skills they will need to lead in the future.

- **Offer Mentorship:** Take the time to mentor future leaders, offering guidance, feedback, and support. Mentorship helps build confidence and ensures that emerging leaders are prepared for their roles.

Leading with Humility

One of the most important qualities of a leader who sustains influence over time is humility. Leaders who lead with humility are more likely to build strong relationships, foster collaboration, and create a lasting impact.

Moses' humility is evident in his willingness to listen to Jethro's advice and make changes to his leadership approach. Rather than clinging to control, Moses recognized that empowering others would not diminish his leadership but would strengthen it. This humility allowed Moses to build a leadership structure that lasted, ensuring that the people of Israel were well served and that his influence endured.

The Role of Humility in Leadership

Humility allows leaders to recognize their limitations, seek input from others, and share the spotlight with their teams. Humble leaders are more approachable, more willing to listen, and more focused on the success of the organization than on their own personal glory.

Practicing Humility

To lead with humility, leaders should:

- **Acknowledge Mistakes:** No leader is perfect. Acknowledging mistakes and learning from them is a sign of strength, not weakness. Leaders who admit their errors build trust with their teams and demonstrate a commitment to continuous improvement.

- **Share Credit:** Humble leaders recognize that success is a team effort. Rather than taking all the credit, they share it with those who contributed to the achievement, fostering a culture of collaboration and mutual respect.
- **Seek Feedback:** Leaders who seek feedback from their teams show that they value input and are open to growth. This creates an environment where continuous improvement is encouraged, and relationships are strengthened.

Creating a Lasting Legacy

Leadership is not just about what happens during a leader's tenure; it's about the impact they leave behind. Leaders who build strong relationships, empower others, and create sustainable systems leave a lasting legacy that endures long after they are gone.

Moses' legacy as a leader was not only the exodus from Egypt but also the leadership structure he put in place, which allowed the Israelites to function as a cohesive community. His decision to delegate and empower others ensured that his leadership would continue to influence the people of Israel for generations.

Conclusion: Sustaining Leadership through Relationships

The story of Moses and Jethro in Exodus 18 offers a powerful example of how leadership can endure through relationships, delegation, and empowerment. By building strong relationships, fostering trust, empowering others, and leading with humility, leaders can sustain their influence and create a lasting legacy. **Leadership that endures** is not about holding onto power; it's about lifting others up, sharing responsibility, and building a foundation for future success.

As you continue your leadership journey, remember that the true measure of leadership is not just in the moment but in the legacy you leave behind. By focusing on relationships, sustainability, and the development of future leaders, you can create a lasting impact that endures for generations.

Longevity in Leadership: Sustaining Influence through Relationships

Leadership that endures goes beyond the actions of one individual; it is about creating a foundation for lasting impact and cultivating a legacy that continues through others. Longevity in leadership doesn't rest on a single person's ability to lead but instead draws from the strength of relationships, delegation, and empowerment. These elements allow leaders to transcend personal limitations and ensure that their influence outlives their tenure.

In a fast-paced world, where changes are constant and challenges are complex, longevity requires leaders to be intentional about building an enduring structure that can withstand both internal and external pressures. Leadership that lasts isn't about holding onto power but rather about nurturing growth in others, sharing responsibility, and establishing a foundation that will support future generations.

The Story of Moses and Jethro: A Model of Sustainable Leadership

The biblical account of Moses and Jethro in *Exodus 18* offers a timeless lesson in sustaining leadership through relationships and shared responsibility. As Moses took on the enormous task of leading the Israelites, he found himself overwhelmed, handling every issue and decision on his own. Jethro, his wise father-in-law, observed the strain Moses was under and advised him to appoint trustworthy leaders to share the responsibilities.

Moses' decision to follow Jethro's advice marked a turning point in his leadership. By delegating authority and empowering others to lead smaller groups, Moses created a structure that allowed for sustainable, long-lasting leadership. This model not only eased his own burden but also gave others a sense of purpose, allowing them to develop and contribute meaningfully to the community. This collaborative leadership structure enabled Moses' influence to reach further than he could have managed alone, creating a legacy of shared leadership and empowerment that served the people for generations.

The Principles of Sustainable Leadership for Modern Leaders

1. Building Strong Relationships

Strong, authentic relationships are the foundation of leadership that endures. Leaders who invest in building relationships with their teams, peers, and other stakeholders cultivate trust and loyalty, which are essential for sustaining influence. These relationships aren't just transactional; they are built on mutual respect, understanding, and shared purpose. When leaders build genuine connections, they create a network of support that can help carry the organization forward, even in challenging times.

Relationships in leadership also extend beyond the leader's immediate circle. By fostering open and inclusive environments, leaders can build connections across the organization. This relational approach helps embed the leader's values and vision into the fabric of the organization, making it more resilient and better prepared to endure over the long term.

2. *Fostering Trust and Transparency*

Trust is the currency of sustainable leadership. Leaders who operate with integrity, honesty, and transparency earn the trust of their teams, which is crucial for sustaining influence. Trust enables leaders to guide their teams through uncertainty, as people are more willing to follow and support leaders they believe in.

Building trust also involves admitting mistakes, being open to feedback, and staying accountable. When leaders are transparent about their intentions, decisions, and challenges, they demonstrate humility and authenticity. This honesty strengthens relationships and creates an environment where team members feel safe to be vulnerable and open, which, in turn, fosters greater collaboration and unity.

3. *Empowering Others and Delegating Responsibility*

Leaders who empower others to lead create a ripple effect that multiplies their influence. Empowerment means trusting team members with responsibility and giving them the authority to make decisions. When leaders empower others, they not only lighten their own workload but also cultivate future leaders who can carry on the organization's mission.

Empowering others also means investing in their growth and development. Leaders who prioritize mentorship and training equip their teams with the skills, knowledge, and confidence to lead effectively. This investment in people creates a legacy of competence and capability, as each empowered individual can, in turn, empower others, ensuring that leadership capacity continues to grow.

Delegation is an essential aspect of empowerment, allowing leaders to focus on strategic matters while enabling others to contribute their expertise. Just as Moses distributed leadership responsibilities among capable leaders, modern leaders should delegate roles in a way that aligns with each individual's strengths. This approach not only boosts productivity but also fosters a sense of ownership and accountability among team members.

4. Leading with Humility and Servant Leadership

Longevity in leadership is rooted in humility. Leaders who are willing to serve others, listen, and learn from their teams create an environment of mutual respect and shared purpose. Humility allows leaders to recognize their limitations, seek support, and prioritize the needs of the organization over personal gain.

Humble leaders understand that leadership is not about control but about service. This servant-leadership mindset builds loyalty, as people are drawn to leaders who genuinely care for their well-being and growth. By leading with humility, leaders create an inclusive culture where everyone feels valued, paving the way for a sustainable legacy that thrives on collective strength.

Creating a Legacy through Relationships and Shared Leadership

The most enduring legacies in leadership are built on relationships, shared vision, and collaborative effort. Leaders who seek to leave a lasting impact focus on developing systems and cultures that can thrive without their direct involvement. This shift from individual leadership to shared leadership ensures that influence is not confined to a single leader but is distributed across the organization.

Succession Planning and Developing Future Leaders

An essential component of sustainable leadership is preparing for succession. Leaders who prioritize succession planning actively identify, train, and mentor potential leaders within their organization. By investing in the next generation, leaders create a pipeline of capable individuals who can continue to uphold the organization's values and mission.

Developing future leaders is more than just identifying successors; it involves creating a culture where leadership is a shared responsibility. When everyone feels empowered to contribute and take initiative, the organization becomes more resilient and adaptable. This culture of shared leadership not only ensures a smooth transition but also strengthens the organization's foundation for continued success.

Embedding Core Values in the Organization's Culture

For leadership to endure, it must be rooted in values that resonate throughout the organization. Leaders who embed core values such as integrity, respect, and collaboration into the organization's culture create a legacy that goes beyond their individual influence. These values act as guiding principles, shaping decision-making and behavior long after the leader has moved on.

A strong values-based culture ensures that everyone, regardless of their role, operates with a sense of shared purpose. This unity fosters resilience and cohesion, as team members are more likely to support one another and work toward common goals. By prioritizing values, leaders lay the groundwork for a legacy that endures and inspires future generations.

Creating Systems for Collaboration and Resilience

Sustainable leadership structures are built on collaboration and resilience. By establishing systems that encourage teamwork, open communication, and shared decision-making, leaders create an organization that can withstand challenges and adapt to change. Just as Moses established a collaborative structure by appointing capable leaders to share his responsibilities, modern leaders can create systems that distribute leadership, enhance resilience, and foster innovation.

Collaborative systems ensure that leadership is not centralized but distributed across various levels. This approach makes the organization more agile, as decisions can be made by those closest to the action. Resilient organizations are less vulnerable to disruptions, as they are supported by multiple leaders who can step up when needed, ensuring continuity and stability.

The Legacy of Sustainable Leadership: Leaving a Lasting Impact

Leadership that endures is not about immediate achievements but about the lasting impact on people, culture, and purpose. Leaders who build strong relationships, foster trust, empower others, and lead with humility leave a legacy that transcends their time in the role. They create organizations that are not only successful but also capable of adapting, evolving, and thriving over time.

For modern leaders, the true measure of success is not in personal accolades but in the foundation they build for others. By focusing on relationships, sustainability, and the development of future leaders, leaders can create a positive and lasting influence that endures for generations. Leadership, in its most meaningful form, is about lifting others up, sharing responsibility, and building a legacy that inspires future leaders to continue the mission with integrity, purpose, and vision.

As you continue your leadership journey, remember that the influence you create today can shape the leaders of tomorrow. By leading with a commitment to relationships, sustainability, and empowerment, you can create a lasting impact that endures far beyond your individual contributions. The true essence of longevity in leadership is not in holding onto power but in empowering others to lead, succeed, and carry forward the legacy you have built.

|Chapter 12|

The Future of Leadership – Why Relationships Will Always Matter

In an age of rapid technological advancement, global interconnectivity, and changing organizational dynamics, leadership continues to evolve. As the world faces increasing complexity, many have wondered if the core principles of leadership will change as well. One thing, however, remains constant: the importance of relationships. Regardless of how much technology transforms communication, work processes, and even leadership itself, the human connection at the heart of leadership remains irreplaceable.

Exodus 18, where Jethro advises Moses, is more than just a historical lesson in delegation. It is a reminder that leadership thrives on relationships—trust, collaboration, and empowerment. These principles are as relevant today as they were in ancient times. While the tools and context of leadership may change, the relational foundation of leadership will always be crucial to success.

In this chapter, we will explore how leadership is changing in a global, technology-driven world and why relationships will continue to be the bedrock of effective leadership. We will look at how leaders can navigate the future while staying grounded in relational leadership principles.

Leadership in the Age of Technology

Technology has transformed the way leaders communicate, make decisions, and interact with their teams. With the rise of artificial intelligence (AI), automation, and remote work, leaders have more tools than ever before to manage their organizations and enhance productivity. However, as technology advances, there is a growing concern that the human aspect of leadership may be lost.

The reality is that while technology can enhance efficiency, streamline processes, and improve data-driven decision-making, it cannot replace the need for strong, authentic relationships. Leaders who rely solely on technology without fostering genuine connections with their teams will struggle to build trust, inspire loyalty, and create a culture of collaboration.

1. Balancing Technology with Human Connection

Leaders of the future must find a balance between leveraging technology and maintaining human connection. While AI and automation can handle many routine tasks, leadership is ultimately about people. Building trust, understanding emotions, and fostering collaboration are all functions of human interaction.

Leaders who effectively balance technology and relationships will use technological tools to support their leadership but will not allow technology to replace meaningful interactions. For example, video conferencing tools like Zoom or Microsoft Teams enable leaders to connect with remote teams, but these interactions still require emotional intelligence, empathy, and active listening.

2. The Rise of Remote Leadership

The global shift toward remote work has been accelerated by the COVID-19 pandemic, and many organizations have adopted hybrid or fully remote work models. This shift has introduced new challenges for leaders, who must now manage teams spread across different time zones and locations.

Remote leadership requires a heightened focus on building relationships. Without the benefit of face-to-face interactions, leaders must be intentional about maintaining regular communication, fostering team cohesion, and ensuring that remote employees feel connected and valued. Leaders who prioritize relationships in a remote environment will build stronger, more resilient teams.

Global Leadership in a Diverse World

As the world becomes increasingly interconnected, leadership is no longer confined to a single country or culture. Global leaders must navigate diverse cultural contexts, manage teams across different regions, and understand the nuances of cross-cultural communication. In this globalized environment, relational leadership is more important than ever.

1. Leading Across Cultures

Cultural diversity enriches teams by bringing different perspectives, ideas, and approaches to problem-solving. However, cultural differences can also create challenges for leaders, particularly when it comes to communication, decision-making, and expectations of authority. Relational leaders understand the importance of cultural sensitivity and make an effort to build relationships that bridge cultural divides.

Leaders who succeed in a global context are those who take the time to learn about the cultures of their team members, respect cultural differences, and adapt their leadership style to meet the needs of diverse teams. They recognize that relationships are at the heart of successful cross-cultural leadership and that building trust across cultural boundaries requires intentionality, empathy, and open-mindedness.

2. The Power of Inclusivity

In the future, leadership will increasingly be defined by its inclusivity. Organizations that embrace diversity and inclusion are more innovative, adaptable, and competitive. However, inclusion is not just about hiring a diverse workforce; it is about creating an environment where everyone feels valued and empowered to contribute.

Relational leaders play a crucial role in fostering inclusivity by building relationships based on respect, trust, and mutual understanding. They actively listen to diverse voices, create opportunities for underrepresented groups, and ensure that everyone has a seat at the table. By cultivating inclusive relationships, leaders create a culture where diversity thrives, and innovation flourishes.

Emotional Intelligence: The Future of Leadership

As technology continues to advance and the global landscape becomes more complex, emotional intelligence (EQ) will become an even more critical leadership skill. In a world where data-driven decision-making is increasingly important, leaders must also be able to connect with people on an emotional level, manage conflicts, and inspire others to achieve their best.

1. Empathy in Leadership Empathy—the ability to understand and share the feelings of others—is at the core of emotional intelligence and relational leadership. Leaders of the future must be able to empathize with their team members, especially in times of change, uncertainty, or crisis. Empathy allows leaders to connect with their teams, understand their needs, and provide the support necessary for them to thrive.

In the future, empathy will be especially important as leaders navigate the challenges of remote work, global collaboration, and rapidly changing environments. Leaders who are empathetic will be better equipped to build trust, resolve conflicts, and foster a positive organizational culture.

2. Emotional Resilience Emotional resilience is the ability to adapt to stressful situations, recover from setbacks, and maintain a positive outlook in the face of adversity. As the pace of change continues to accelerate, leaders will need to develop emotional resilience to navigate the challenges of the future. This includes managing their own emotions, staying calm under pressure, and providing a steady, reassuring presence for their teams.

Leaders with high emotional intelligence are more likely to be emotionally resilient. They are able to manage stress, remain focused on long-term goals, and help their teams stay motivated, even in the face of uncertainty.

The Enduring Power of Relationships In a rapidly changing world, one thing remains constant: leadership is fundamentally about relationships. Whether leading a small team, a global corporation, or a community organization, the ability to build and maintain strong relationships will always be the foundation of effective leadership.

1. Relationships Drive Results Leaders who prioritize relationships over tasks are more likely to achieve sustainable, long-term success. Strong relationships foster collaboration, trust, and engagement, all of which drive performance. In contrast, leaders who focus solely on tasks and results without investing in relationships often find that their influence is short-lived.

In the future, leaders who build meaningful relationships with their teams, colleagues, and stakeholders will be better positioned to navigate the complexities of global leadership and achieve lasting results.

2. Relationships Create Legacy Leadership is not just about what happens during a leader's tenure; it's about the impact they leave behind. Leaders who invest in relationships create a legacy that endures long after they are gone. Their influence continues through the people they have mentored, the teams they have built, and the cultures they have shaped.

In Exodus 18, Moses' legacy as a leader was not only in the exodus itself but in the leadership structure he created. By appointing leaders over smaller groups and delegating responsibility, Moses ensured that his leadership would endure beyond his individual capacity. This relational approach to leadership allowed for the continued growth and success of the Israelite community.

Conclusion

Leading into the Future with Relationships at the Core As we look to the future of leadership, it's clear that technology, globalization, and cultural shifts will continue to shape the way leaders operate. However, the core principles of relational leadership will remain timeless. Leaders who prioritize relationships—building trust, fostering collaboration, and leading with empathy—will continue to thrive in the face of change.

Leadership that lasts is leadership that is grounded in relationships. The future may bring new challenges and opportunities, but the leaders who succeed will be those who understand that their greatest asset is not technology or strategy but the people they lead.

As you navigate the future of leadership, remember that relationships are the foundation of everything. By investing in your relationships, developing emotional intelligence, and leading with empathy and inclusivity, you can create a legacy of leadership that endures for generations to come.

The Future of Leadership: Why Relationships Will Always Win The world is advancing rapidly, with technology, globalization, and cultural shifts reshaping the landscape of leadership. Yet, amid these profound changes, the fundamental aspects of relational leadership will continue to be indispensable. While tools, systems, and strategies may evolve, the human connection remains irreplaceable. Leaders who understand that people are their most valuable asset will be better equipped to thrive in an increasingly complex world.

The leaders of tomorrow must therefore embrace relational leadership as the key to enduring success. This approach prioritizes trust, collaboration, empathy, and emotional intelligence, equipping leaders to respond with resilience, adaptability, and compassion—qualities that technology alone cannot replace. Leadership grounded in relationships is not only sustainable; it's the foundation for creating a legacy that lasts.

Technology, Globalization, and Cultural Shifts: The Future Landscape of Leadership As technology becomes more integrated into every aspect of work, leaders have access to a range of tools to streamline processes, analyze data, and facilitate communication. However, while technology can enhance efficiency and decision-making, it cannot replicate the depth of human relationships. Leaders who rely solely on digital systems to connect with people may miss out on the nuances of interpersonal interactions and the genuine connections that build trust.

Globalization is also transforming the workforce, bringing together individuals from diverse cultures, backgrounds, and experiences. This diversity offers tremendous potential for innovation and creativity, but it also requires leaders to be culturally sensitive, inclusive, and empathetic. Relational leadership skills, such as emotional intelligence and empathy, become crucial as leaders navigate these diverse perspectives and create an environment where everyone feels valued.

Cultural shifts are redefining workplace expectations, with an increasing focus on inclusion, work-life balance, and purpose-driven work. Modern employees seek meaningful work and leaders who respect their individuality and well-being. Leaders who prioritize relationships are better positioned to meet these expectations, fostering a supportive culture that resonates with the aspirations of their team members.

- Relational Leadership: The Timeless Approach for Future Success

1. **Building Trust in a Fast-Changing World** Trust is the foundation of any relationship, and it will be even more critical in the future as leaders face the complexities of a globalized, technology-driven world. Leaders who cultivate trust can guide their teams through change with greater ease, as people are more willing to follow leaders they trust. Trust builds loyalty and resilience, which are essential for adapting to new challenges.

Building trust in the future will require consistency, transparency, and authenticity. Leaders must communicate openly about their decisions, involve their teams in the process, and demonstrate integrity in all interactions. Trust isn't built overnight; it requires sustained effort. Leaders who prioritize it create a foundation that enables their teams to take risks, innovate, and collaborate openly.

2. Fostering Collaboration across Boundaries The future of leadership will rely heavily on collaboration, often across geographical, cultural, and functional boundaries. Relational leaders understand that the strength of a team lies in the diverse perspectives and skills of its members. By fostering a culture of collaboration, leaders can harness these strengths to

solve complex problems, innovate, and achieve shared goals.

Collaboration in a globalized context requires cultural sensitivity and a willingness to embrace different viewpoints. Leaders must create spaces for dialogue, encourage participation from all team members, and celebrate diverse contributions. Collaborative leaders break down silos, promote cross-functional interaction, and ensure that everyone feels included in the organization's mission. This approach not only strengthens the team but also builds a resilient organization that can adapt to new challenges.

3. Leading with Empathy and Emotional Intelligence As the pace of change accelerates, emotional intelligence (EI) becomes a cornerstone of effective leadership. Relational leaders who lead with empathy can better understand the needs, concerns, and aspirations of their teams, creating an environment where people feel valued and supported. Empathy allows leaders to connect with people on a personal level, even in a high-tech, fast-paced environment.

Leaders with high EI can manage their own emotions, respond thoughtfully to stress, and navigate difficult conversations with compassion. This skill is essential as workplaces become more diverse and as leaders work with teams across various cultural and generational backgrounds. By leading with empathy, leaders build strong relationships, resolve conflicts constructively, and foster a sense of unity and purpose.

4. Investing in People Development and Growth The future of leadership is not about controlling or directing every aspect of work; it's about empowering others to lead, succeed, and innovate. Leaders who

invest in their people—providing mentorship, training, and opportunities for growth—create a legacy of empowerment. This investment in people is a long-term strategy that yields high returns as individuals grow into leaders themselves.

Developing others requires patience, encouragement, and a commitment to the success of each team member. Relational leaders understand that by empowering others, they multiply their impact and create a sustainable leadership pipeline. This approach fosters loyalty and engagement, as people feel valued and recognized for their potential.

Creating a Culture of Inclusivity and Belonging

Inclusivity will be central to the future of leadership as leaders work with teams that reflect a wide range of backgrounds, experiences, and perspectives. Relational leaders recognize that inclusivity goes beyond token gestures; it's about creating a culture where everyone feels they belong and can contribute authentically. Leaders who prioritize inclusivity demonstrate respect for each individual's unique strengths and encourage collaboration across differences.

Inclusive leaders are aware of biases, actively seek input from underrepresented voices, and ensure that everyone has equal opportunities to contribute and succeed. This approach builds a more innovative and dynamic organization, as diverse perspectives lead to richer ideas and solutions. By fostering a culture of inclusivity, leaders can create a workplace where people feel motivated and supported to do their best work.

The Timeless Value of Relational Leadership

In a future marked by rapid change, the principles of relational leadership will remain timeless. Leaders who prioritize relationships—those who lead with empathy, build trust, and foster collaboration—will be better prepared to face the challenges and opportunities that lie ahead. Relational leadership is adaptable, resilient, and deeply human, making it the ideal approach for navigating the complexities of a global, interconnected world.

1. Resilience through Relationships

Strong relationships create a resilient foundation for any organization. Teams that trust and respect each other are more capable of adapting to change, overcoming challenges, and supporting each other in times of uncertainty. Relational leaders build resilience by fostering open communication, encouraging collaboration, and promoting a sense of shared purpose.

2. Adaptability in an Ever-Evolving Environment

The future will require leaders to be highly adaptable, and relational leadership naturally supports this flexibility. By staying attuned to the needs and perspectives of their teams, relational leaders can respond to change in a way that honors and supports their people. This adaptability is crucial as technological advancements, cultural shifts, and global events continue to reshape the world.

3. Legacy through Lasting Relationships

The true measure of leadership is not only in the accomplishments achieved during one's tenure but in the legacy left behind. Leaders who invest in relationships create a foundation for future success, as their influence extends through the people they've inspired, mentored, and empowered. By focusing on relationships, relational leaders leave a legacy of trust, respect, and collaboration—a legacy that endures beyond their individual contributions.

Leading into the Future: Relationships as the Foundation of Lasting Success

As leaders look to the future, it's clear that relationships will remain at the heart of effective leadership. Technology and strategy are valuable tools, but they cannot replace the depth and power of human connection. Leadership that lasts is grounded in relationships because people—not tools, systems, or trends—are what ultimately drive success.

To lead effectively in the future, leaders must continue to prioritize relationships. By investing in their connections, developing emotional intelligence, and leading with empathy and inclusivity, leaders can create environments where people feel valued, motivated, and united by a common purpose. Relational leadership is not just a way to navigate the challenges of today; it's a pathway to building a legacy that endures for generations to come. As you continue your leadership journey, remember that the foundation of leadership is, and always will be, the relationships you build. This investment in people is the key to creating a future of leadership that is both impactful and enduring.

Conclusion: Leadership That Endures

As we draw this journey to a close, it's important to reflect on the timeless principles of leadership that we have explored. Leadership is not just about achieving success or reaching milestones—it is about creating a lasting impact through the people you lead. At the heart of this impact is the fundamental truth: leadership thrives on relationships. Whether we are drawing lessons from the biblical story of Moses and Jethro or looking at modern leadership challenges, the principles remain constant. Relationships are the foundation upon which enduring leadership is built.

The Relational Leadership Journey

In Exodus 18, we saw how Moses' leadership evolved when he embraced the advice of Jethro, delegating responsibilities and empowering others to lead. This transformation not only made his leadership more sustainable but also strengthened the community he served. Moses' shift to relational leadership—marked by trust, delegation, empathy, and shared responsibility—ensured that his influence endured long after his individual capacity was reached.

As leaders in today's complex, globalized world, we face the same challenge: how to lead effectively, sustainably, and with lasting impact. The answer lies in relationships. By prioritizing the people around us, fostering trust, and empowering others, we can build leadership structures that are resilient and adaptive to the ever-changing demands of the future.

Key Lessons from the Journey

1. **Leadership is Rooted in People, Not Processes:** While systems, strategies, and structures are important, the

essence of leadership is the ability to influence, inspire, and guide people. The success of any leader is directly tied to their ability to build meaningful, authentic relationships.

2. **Delegation is Key to Sustainability:** As we learned from Jethro's counsel to Moses, trying to do everything yourself leads to burnout and limits your impact. Delegation is not a sign of weakness but a mark of wisdom. By empowering others and sharing responsibility, leaders can focus on the areas where their influence is most needed while allowing others to grow in their leadership roles.
3. **Emotional Intelligence Fuels Leadership Success:** Effective leadership requires emotional intelligence—the ability to understand and manage your own emotions while connecting empathetically with others. Leaders who are emotionally intelligent foster trust, build strong teams, and navigate challenges with resilience.
4. **Cultural Sensitivity and Inclusivity Are Essential in Global Leadership:** In today's interconnected world, leaders must be able to navigate cultural differences and lead diverse teams. Relational leaders understand that inclusivity and respect for different perspectives are essential for creating an environment where innovation and collaboration can thrive.
5. **Longevity in Leadership Comes from Mentorship and Empowerment:** The leaders who leave a lasting legacy are those who invest in others. By mentoring future leaders, empowering teams, and fostering a

culture of shared leadership, leaders ensure that their influence continues long after they have moved on.

The Legacy of Relational Leadership

The true legacy of leadership is not found in titles, accolades, or power. It is found in the lives of the people you have touched, the leaders you have developed, and the relationships you have built. When leadership is rooted in relationships, it creates a ripple effect that spreads far beyond the individual leader, impacting teams, organizations, and even entire communities.

Moses' legacy was not just the liberation of the Israelites but the leadership structure he established that allowed them to thrive as a community. Similarly, the legacy of modern leaders will be measured not by individual accomplishments but by the strength of the relationships they have built and the leaders they have empowered.

Looking Forward: Leading into the Future

The future of leadership will undoubtedly bring new challenges—technological advancements, cultural shifts, and global uncertainties. However, the principles of relational leadership will remain timeless. Leaders who prioritize relationships, embrace emotional intelligence, and foster collaboration will continue to thrive in the face of change.

As you move forward in your leadership journey, remember that the foundation of your influence is built on the relationships you cultivate. By investing in people, leading with empathy, and empowering others, you will create a leadership legacy that endures, leaving a lasting impact on those you lead.

Final Thoughts

In the end, leadership is not about how much power or authority you have but about how you use your influence to lift others up, inspire greatness, and create a positive impact. Leadership thrives on relationships, and as long as you make those relationships the core of your leadership philosophy, your influence will extend far beyond your time in any particular role.

Take to heart the wisdom of Jethro and the example of Moses: recognize your limitations, seek counsel, delegate responsibilities, and build a leadership structure that empowers others. By doing so, you will not only achieve success but also create a leadership legacy that lasts for generations.

Lead with relationships, lead with empathy, and lead with the future in mind. This is the path to leadership that truly endures.

Some powerful quotes by renowned thinkers, authors, and leaders on the importance of relationships in leadership:
These quotes capture the essence of how relationships are central to effective leadership, emphasizing the power of trust, connection, influence, and empathy in guiding and inspiring others.

1. **John C. Maxwell**

"Leadership is not about titles, positions, or flowcharts. It is about one life influencing another."

2. **Simon Sinek**

"A team is not a group of people that work together. A team is a group of people that trust each other."

3. **Peter Drucker**
"The most important thing in communication is hearing what isn't said."

4. **Robin Sharma**
"The business of business is relationships; the business of life is human connection."

5. **Stephen Covey**
"When the trust account is high, communication is easy, instant, and effective."

6. **Ken Blanchard**
"The key to successful leadership today is influence, not authority."

7. **Warren Bennis**
"Leadership is the capacity to translate vision into reality. It's built on trust, integrity, and genuine connections."
8. **Brené Brown**
"Connection is why we're here; it is what gives purpose and meaning to our lives."

9. **Jim Rohn**
"One person caring about another represents life's greatest value."

10. **Margaret Wheatley**

"Relationships are all there is. Everything in the universe only exists because it is in relationship to everything else. Nothing exists in isolation."

11. **Howard Schultz**
"When you're surrounded by people who share a passionate commitment around a common purpose, anything is possible."

12. **Marshall Goldsmith**
"Great leaders build great relationships and achieve great results by caring more about the people they lead."

13. **Vineet Nayar**
"Empowering those around you to be heard and valued makes the difference between a leader who simply instructs and one who inspires."

14. **Patrick Lencioni**
"Teamwork begins by building trust. And the only way to do that is to overcome our need for invulnerability."

15. **John Wooden**
"The most powerful leadership tool you have is your own personal example."

A to Z of Salvation

The journey of salvation is both profound and life-changing. It is a step-by-step process that leads us to a deeper relationship with God and a transformed life in Christ. Below is a guide to the A to Z of salvation, with accompanying scriptures to illuminate each step.

A: Agree That You Are a Sinner
"For all have sinned and fall short of the glory of God." — Romans 3:23
Acknowledging your need for salvation begins with recognizing that sin has separated you from God. This step humbles your heart and opens the way for repentance.

B: Believe That Jesus Christ Came to Save You
"If you declare with your mouth, 'Jesus is Lord,' and believe in your heart that God raised Him from the dead, you will be saved." — Romans 10:9
Salvation is rooted in faith—believing that Jesus died for your sins and rose again to give you eternal life.

C: Confess Jesus Christ as Your Savior
"For it is with your heart that you believe and are justified, and it is with your mouth that you profess your faith and are saved." — Romans 10:10

Confessing Jesus as your Savior publicly acknowledges your faith and solidifies your commitment to follow Him.

D: Desire a Walk of Fellowship

"God is faithful, who has called you into fellowship with His Son, Jesus Christ our Lord." — 1 Corinthians 1:9

Salvation is not the end but the beginning of a lifelong journey of fellowship with Christ. Develop a longing to walk closely with Him daily.

E: Encounter the Holy Spirit

"But you will receive power when the Holy Spirit comes on you; and you will be my witnesses." — Acts 1:8

The Holy Spirit empowers, guides, and comforts believers. Seek to experience His presence and let Him lead you in your walk with Christ.

F: Find a Community of Believers

"They devoted themselves to the apostles' teaching and to fellowship, to the breaking of bread and to prayer." — Acts 2:42

A supportive community of believers strengthens your faith, provides accountability, and encourages spiritual growth.

G: Grow in the Word of God

"Like newborn babies, crave pure spiritual milk, so that by it you may grow up in your salvation." — 1 Peter 2:2

Regular study of God's Word deepens your understanding of His will and equips you to live a Christ-centered life.

H: Hope in Eternal Life

"He has saved us and called us to a holy life... because of His own purpose and grace." — 2 Timothy 1:9

Salvation gives us hope, not only for this life but for eternity with God. Let this hope inspire your daily walk.

I: Imitate Christ's Character

"Follow God's example, therefore, as dearly loved children." — Ephesians 5:1

Salvation transforms us into the likeness of Christ. Strive to reflect His love, humility, and holiness in all you do.

J: Join in Service to Others

"For we are God's handiwork, created in Christ Jesus to do good works." — Ephesians 2:10

As a saved person, you are called to serve others with the love and gifts God has given you.

K: Keep the Faith

"Fight the good fight of the faith. Take hold of the eternal life to which you were called." — 1 Timothy 6:12

Salvation is sustained through unwavering faith, especially in trials. Hold fast to God's promises.

L: Live a Life of Love

"And now these three remain: faith, hope, and love. But the greatest of these is love." — 1 Corinthians 13:13

Love is the evidence of salvation. Let Christ's love flow through you to touch others.

M: Meditate on God's Word

"Blessed is the one... whose delight is in the law of the Lord, and who meditates on His law day and night." — Psalm 1:1-2

Meditating on Scripture keeps your heart aligned with God's will and renews your mind daily.

N: Nurture Your Spiritual Gifts

"We have different gifts, according to the grace given to each of us." — Romans 12:6

Discover and use your spiritual gifts to glorify God and edify the Church.

O: Obey God's Commandments

"If you love me, keep my commands." — John 14:15

Obedience is the fruit of a transformed heart. It demonstrates your love for God and commitment to His ways.

P: Pray Without Ceasing

"Pray continually." — 1 Thessalonians 5:17

Prayer is vital for communication with God. It strengthens your relationship with Him and aligns your will with His.

Q: Quench Not the Spirit

"Do not quench the Spirit." — 1 Thessalonians 5:19

Remain sensitive to the Holy Spirit's guidance and avoid anything that grieves or silences Him.

R: Repent Daily

"If we confess our sins, He is faithful and just and will forgive us our sins." — 1 John 1:9

Though saved, believers still fall short. Daily repentance keeps your heart clean and your relationship with God strong.

S: Share the Gospel

"Go into all the world and preach the gospel to all creation." — Mark 16:15

Salvation compels you to share the Good News with others, inviting them into the family of God.

T: Trust in the Lord Always

"Trust in the Lord with all your heart and lean not on your own understanding." — Proverbs 3:5

Faith in God's sovereignty and goodness sustains you in every season of life.

U: Understand God's Grace

"But He said to me, 'My grace is sufficient for you, for my power is made perfect in weakness.'" — 2 Corinthians 12:9

God's grace is the foundation of salvation. Embrace it fully, knowing it covers all your shortcomings.

V: Victory through Christ

"But thanks be to God! He gives us the victory through our Lord Jesus Christ." — 1 Corinthians 15:57

Through Christ, you have victory over sin, death, and the powers of darkness.

W: Worship the Lord

"Worship the Lord in the splendor of His holiness." — Psalm 96:9

Worship is an essential response to salvation, expressing gratitude and adoration for God.

X: Examine Yourself Regularly

"Examine yourselves to see whether you are in the faith." — 2 Corinthians 13:5

Self-reflection ensures that you are walking in alignment with God's will and growing in faith.

Y: Yield to God's Will

"Submit yourselves, then, to God. Resist the devil, and he will flee from you." — James 4:7

Yielding to God's will allows Him to work powerfully in and through you.

Z: Zealously Pursue God's Kingdom

"Never be lacking in zeal, but keep your spiritual fervor, serving the Lord." — Romans 12:11

A passion for God's kingdom fuels your commitment to live for His glory and advance His purposes.

This A to Z guide to salvation encapsulates the essence of a Christ-centered life. Each step, grounded in Scripture, builds a strong foundation for your faith and empowers you to live in the fullness of God's promises.